Buttermilk and Dragonflies

Other Books By Mary R. Hemmer

Phe and the Work of Death (under Mary R. H. Demmler name)

In the Beginning Was The Word: An Anthology,
Katerina Katsarka Whitley, ed. (Mary R. Hemmer, contributor)
All proceeds from this book go to support the Valle Crucis
Conference Center in Valle Crucis, North Carolina

Buttermilk and Dragonflies

Reflections from Ordinary Time

Mary R. Hemmer

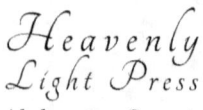
Alpharetta, Georgia

Although the author and publisher have made every effort to ensure that the information in this book was correct at the time of first publication, the author and publisher do not assume and hereby disclaim any liability to any party for any loss, damage, or disruption caused by errors or omissions, whether such errors or omissions result from negligence, accident, or any other cause.

Copyright © 2024 by Mary R. Hemmer

All rights reserved. No part of this book may be reproduced or transmitted in any form or by any means, electronic or mechanical, including photocopying, recording, or any information storage and retrieval system, without permission in writing from the author.

ISBN: 978-1-6653-0975-2 – Paperback
eISBN: 978-1-6653-0976-9 – eBook

These ISBNs are the property of Heavenly Light Press (a Division of BookLogix) for the express purpose of sales and distribution of this title. The content of this book is the property of the copyright holder only. Heavenly Light Press does not hold any ownership of the content of this book and is not liable in any way for the materials contained within. The views and opinions expressed in this book are the property of the Author/Copyright holder, and do not necessarily reflect those of Heavenly Light Press/BookLogix.

Library of Congress Control Number: 2024922209

♾This paper meets the requirements of ANSI/NISO Z39.48-1992 (Permanence of Paper)

103024

*For my three dragonflies, R., B., and W.,
who show me the extraordinary in the ordinary every day.*

Contents

Introduction: Rainbows and Prisms   ix

Extraordinarily Ordinary	1
The Seriousness of the Youngest Disciples	6
For the Sport of It	11
The Prodigal and the Pigs	15
Prayer in the Kitchen	20
For Rosemary	25
God the Father and Father's Day…It's Complicated.	31
The Error in Fundamentals	34
Sacrificing Busyness	37
Homemade Butter and the Drip, Dripping of Sabbath Time	41
Faith in Stitches	45
Jesus Wept, So Why Can't We?	48
Gratitude in Offering	51
Consider the Dandelion	55
Standing in My Sun	58
Enzymes and Hospitality	62
Hope in the Face of a Ring Bearer	66
I'm Sorry, I Can't.	70
Bumper Cars and Spider Webs	74
Savor	78
The Unbearable, Relatable All-Or-Nothing of Peter	82
A Good Word Not for Me	86
Loving the Story, Inspiring Play	92
Not Your Time. Not Your Place. Not Your Call.	96
WWJD? WWID?	103

Bob Ross and Waiting to Understand Jesus   107
A Dragonfly's Wings   113

Acknowledgments   *117*
Index: Reflections by Theme   *119*

Introduction
Rainbows and Prisms

Holy Scripture is like a prism: it is not God or even Ultimate Truth, but it does capture the light of Truth, reflecting it in different ways. The prism patterns of light cast on the ceiling, walls, and faces of those who delight in its abilities change and shift as you turn the prism over in your hand. So, too, the way we view and understand God shifts as we turn over the prism of Scripture to look at it in different ways. As the events of our lives push us to grow and mature, our connection with the Bible evolves with us. A passage that overwhelmed us at a younger age no longer carries the same punch as we age; after we survive some of life's more significant challenges, biblical verses that rang empty to us in our youth suddenly hold the key to a deeper connection with the divine.

I wish I could claim this description for myself. I first heard this description of Holy Scripture from Rabbi Mark Biller from New Jersey. A colleague and friend invited Rabbi Biller to speak at a symposium hosted by her church. I joined as a leader for a breakout session, which granted me access to his talks and the panel discussion with all the leaders. During a Q&A, one of the participants asked the Rabbi about the inerrancy of Scripture; he provided this beautiful analogy as an answer.

Not one understanding of Scripture can hold the whole truth of God. In reality, we turn the prism of Scripture over and over again throughout human history and still only capture a fraction of the divine in our combined perspectives. If we grasp the Bible too tightly, we choose the account of one witness to represent the whole story. Actually, it's worse than that. Any interpretation we receive today comes from the interpretations of interpretations. Even the Gospels represent secondhand and thirdhand accounts of the life of Christ. Two thousand years later, we hear preachers, theologians, scholars, and pastors reflect on these varied accounts through translations that are also interpreted from the original language. Translators must decide which English word best matches the koine Greek or ancient Hebrew. Writers of the Christian Scripture employed four different words that we translate as "love." By virtue of the limitations of the English language in describing "love," we lose some of the meaning inherent in the original text.

Just as Scripture captures and reflects beautifully and imperfectly divine truth, so does each of us. We process God through our experiences, learning, lenses of culture and family, and unique epiphanies. The prism I hold does not mirror yours, nor should it. You do not encounter God the same as I, nor has your life followed the same path as mine. Even identical twins look at the world through different sets of eyes.

This book contains reflections on faith filtered through my lens as an Episcopal priest, a mother, a once-Baptist, a Southerner, a daughter, a co-parent, a partner, and more. My life mixes the ingredients of the many roles I have and do play, tossing in a pinch of this and a dash of that every day. I don't think I'll ever be fully baked; at least, I hope not. Since Christ promises eternal life, I pray I never stop learning or experiencing revelations, even long past my early expiration date.

This particular collection comes from my encounters with the divine during Ordinary Time. In churches that follow the traditional liturgical calendar, "Ordinary Time" makes up the bulk of the church year, and we signify it by wearing green vestments. We have a few weeks of it from Epiphany to Ash Wednesday, but then a long stretch comes from Pentecost to the start of Advent and the new year. This is a time outside the seasons. I like to think of it as "the rest of the story." As a little girl, I listened to the radio in my father's car as he shuttled me from school to various practices to home. He loved Paul Harvey's radio show, and I learned to look forward to Harvey's singular voice proclaiming, "And THAT is the rest of the story." Such a fantastic tag line and closing for his show. The end of each episode carried a surprise of some sort that felt like his way of saying, "Gotcha!"

During Ordinary Time, we hear the non-seasonal stories of Christ's life, including his many lessons and teachings, his interactions with his disciples, and his miracles. We cannot celebrate Christmas and Easter every day, nor would we want to spend fifty-two Sundays wading through the heaviness of Lent and Holy Week. The rest of the time, we relax into the stories introducing us to Jesus, the man who broke bread with his friends, the miracle worker who healed with the slightest touch, and the Messiah who walked on water. I love to decorate my home for major holidays and feast on special foods, but I need the predictable pattern of "regular" life between, and I feel the same about our long stretches of Ordinary Time in the church.

I pray this book becomes a companion on your journey through the long green season, a term often used to refer to Ordinary Time in the liturgical calendar. I also pray you agree and disagree with me in turns. Your prism won't reflect God's light as mine does, and you might find contradictory patterns between us. That's as it should be! If you find a point you want to argue or if you want to share an epiphany, find me on my website or blog and comment or send me a message. My understanding of the divine deepens whenever I get to glimpse God from someone else's perspective; I hope this book will do the same for you.

A note on pronouns: You'll see in this book that I use both "He" and "She" to refer to God. Genesis 1:27 states, "God created humanity in God's own image, in the divine image God created them, male and female God created them." (Common English translation). I prefer using both pronouns when referring to the divine to remind myself and others of this fact. One single gender cannot represent the divine, and this includes all that exist on the gender spectrum. We all benefit from using different pronouns (or none) to refer to God; this is a sure preventative against misogyny and bigotry.

A note on translations: I prefer the accuracy of the New Revised Standard Version, though I often cite the Common English translation as well. Unless otherwise stated, I have used the NRSV when quoting scripture.

Extraordinarily Ordinary

For years, I have dreamed of hosting a podcast on which I speak with friends whom the world would call "ordinary" but whom I find extraordinary. None of them claim any fame or notoriety. Their friends and family know them, and maybe some strangers on social media but otherwise, they pass through their days unrecognized by passersby. These "normal" people have extraordinary experiences, unique perspectives, and marvelous stories. Should I ever get around to creating such a podcast, I will call it "extraordinarily ordinary."

    A friend of mine worked all through high school and during summers home from college in an ice cream parlor. She scooped up fancy flavors, combining caramel with chocolate chunks and pretzel pieces, or strawberries with white chocolate swirl and graham cracker crumbs. I once asked her how often people ordered chocolate or vanilla as opposed to one of the more involved flavors. She told me people chose chocolate more than vanilla, but I would be surprised by how many people did want "just" vanilla. She also mentioned how those customers faced teasing by their companions for not being more inspired in their ordering.

Vanilla seems ordinary when stacked against rocky road, moose tracks, or turtle pecan cluster crunch. People who say they prefer vanilla over any other kind of ice cream often do so apologetically, a sure sign of years of ridicule. But vanilla provides the base for so many other creations. It lays the foundation for nearly every other flavor, even if we deem it too ordinary to be someone's favorite.

The Episcopal Church follows the ancient liturgical calendar, through which the seasons take us from Advent to Christmas to Epiphany. Lent leads to Easter and Pentecost, stopping for a Trinity Sunday and All Saints Observance before ending grandly with Christ the King Sunday. We love the seasons of the church, and so does the secular world. Non-Christians and Christians alike buy red and green decorations in December for their porches and tables, and fluffy bunnies with colored eggs cover lawns and shop windows alike in the spring. The seasons bring excitement and needed breaks in our otherwise mundane lives. We cook special meals, exchange gifts, listen to prescribed seasonal music, and make a more concerted effort to see friends and family. I admit that even in July, I feel giddy about Christmas and dream of peppermint ice cream.

But between all of those seasons, from Epiphany to Ash Wednesday, and then from Pentecost to the end of the liturgical calendar, we observe non-season periods that we call "ordinary time." The church assigns green as the color for those periods, and many Episcopalians grow weary of seeing all that green for such long stretches. When parishioners return from a long vacation away in the Fall, I have heard their exclamation upon returning to the familiar worship space: "Ugh! Green still?" However, 'Ordinary Time' is not about boredom or routine. It's a time for growth, reflection, and living out our faith in the everyday. It's a time to find the extraordinary in the ordinary, providing the plain vanilla foundation of our faith.

As a member of the Episcopal Church, I've often found myself in the 'Ordinary Time' periods wishing for the chaotic energy of the seasons. We hear "ordinary time" and think, "Oh, so boring." The Revised Common Lectionary fills our Sundays with stories from the Hebrew Scriptures in chronological order, and then shows us the daily workings of Jesus's life in the gospels—his birth, baptism, and murder on the cross. The rest of the story stretches out with the long weeks of this time between the critical seasons, ones that show us the daily life of Jesus and his disciples—important lessons, even if we prefer the drama of the seasons and the unique feelings the seasons ignite in us.

Yet, the stories of Ordinary Time are far from average. They are the stories of Jesus feeding the multitude, walking on water, and healing the sick. He preaches a sermon on a mount that shapes our faith, and we learn through these stories how God wants us to behave in the world and with one another. We should not find anything plain or boring in Christ's parables and interactions with others. These periods of non-seasons are extraordinarily ordinary, and they hold a wealth of wisdom and significance.

The term "ordinary time" actually doesn't have anything to do with how we use the term "ordinary" in our modern context. It does not mean that these periods are average or typical. We do not perceive it as boring or routine. "Ordinary," in this case, means "ordinal" for the way we count those Sundays. For instance, we say the "third Sunday after Epiphany" or the "fourteenth Sunday after Pentecost." This differs from seasonal Sundays called the "Second Sunday in Advent" or the "Third Sunday in Easter." Sundays in seasons belong to those seasons, whereas in Ordinary Time, we merely count the Sundays and assign readings to them. "Ordinal numbering" refers simply to how we count things as first, second, third, fourth, and so on.

In Ordinary Time, we count the Sundays and, so, count time. This could be akin to counting the seconds on a clock until the last bell rings before school lets out or counting the minutes until a loved one steps off a plane and makes their way to the arrivals lounge. The old adage "A watched pot never boils" warns us of counting time and wasting it in waiting. We do not enjoy counting time, preferring action and activity.

How often do we count down or up to pass the time in our lives? We count to nine as we await a baby's arrival. We count to ten, then run to seek friends hiding around the house. Days and weeks mark how long we must wait for test results in order to figure out a course of treatment. High school seniors check their emails hourly, sometimes in anticipation of an acceptance letter from their college of choice. Retirement comes, and soon-to-be retirees watch the days on the calendar march to their final day at work, feeling relief and trepidation.

We think of this counting as waiting and watching, a time without time, sometimes flying by and other times dragging. I despise transitions, hating the space between one thing ending and another beginning. When I have completed or nearly completed a task or assignment, the racehorses in my mind knock their hooves against the starting gate, growing increasingly agitated as they wait for newness and the novelty of beginnings. We become antsy in checkout lines, so we hop on our phones to feel productive in some way while waiting for our turn.

In the meantime, the world spins around us, and activity buzzes during this time of sitting and doing nothing. Ordinary time, the act of counting Sundays, walks us through some of the more beautiful teachings of Christ, the ones we need for our everyday existence and not just for special occasions. I may not need to be reminded hourly how God forgives me, but I do need the reminder to love my neighbor as myself almost by the minute. At some point in every day, I don't recall the power of my baptism, but I do feel the abundance of God's love and mercy.

We live most of our lives in the plain vanilla periods. Not every season can be Christmas or filled with wedding showers or fireworks. We mark the passage of days through the bulk of our lives, not with carols, but by singing old songs and learning new ones, none of which connects to a baby or palms. These ordinary days bring us extraordinary moments, exceptional surprises, and unexpected lessons.

Throughout the pages of this book, you will find some of those moments from my life as I have served as an Episcopal priest, raised three children, managed a family farm, and spent more than a few hours in the kitchen. I don't succeed in finding the extraordinary in the ordinary every day—truthfully, I fail to do so most of my days. But I strive to keep my ears open and my antennae up, hoping that when I tear my eyes away from the about-to-boil pot I will notice the hummingbirds buzzing by my kitchen window. Maybe, I'll dip into my freezer for a bowl of vanilla bean ice cream, then sit on the porch to watch them.

The Seriousness of the Youngest Disciples

Many years ago, in my first position as a priest, I served a tiny congregation in South Georgia, one that included established local families and those of Air Force officers from the nearby base. Long-time members welcomed transient ones, helping them to settle into the community and church family as quickly as possible. We loved it when these military families arrived, even if we knew we would have them for less than five years. The parents volunteered quickly for parish workdays and potluck suppers while their children brought bright energy to our small fold.

One Sunday, I stood at the altar rail, waiting for worshippers to come forward for communion as they do every Sunday. The organist played softly as each person knelt and held a time of reflection while waiting for me to place a piece of the blessed bread in their outstretched palms. During this time those kneeling usually hold a solemn space for prayer. Occasionally, people smile and mouth "hello" to one another but, otherwise, Episcopalians like to stay quiet as they receive the body and blood of Christ.

A family new to the congregation brought their four-year-old forward, dangling off his mother's arm as they stepped forward and knelt. He watched with wide eyes as his parents bowed their heads and put forward their hands, and he did the same. I could see his gaze cutting around the rail to see others, to ensure he participated correctly in this strange performance. I placed the host in his hands and watched as he giggled and took a gulp of wine from the cup offered by the chalice bearer. He squeezed his eyes shut and then licked his lips. His parents took his hands in theirs and turned from the altar. They had taken about two steps when we all heard the most glorious belch usher from the little boy. Needless to say, no one could maintain a reflective silence as we all giggled. Oblivious to our reaction, the little boy tugged at the arms of his red-faced parents, eager to return to his seat and his little pile of toys. For me, he offered the most marvelous affirmation of the satisfaction of communion with this boisterous burp.

Another time, at this same church, a nine-year-old came forward with his mother only to leave the rail confused and somewhat suspicious of my offering to him. In many Episcopal churches, the priest blesses a large round host (thin cracker-like bread) that can be broken into a dozen or more smaller pieces as well as a plate of individual small hosts. The priest generally gives people one of the smaller wafers, but some worshippers receive a piece broken off the priest's. I gave the mother one of the individual hosts but offered the son a piece broken off of the priest's host. I watched him frown a little, then look at his mom's hands before looking back at his own. He lifted the broken piece to his mouth with a disappointed air.

After the service, the mother came to me smiling. The son had seen his broken piece, compared it to his mother's whole smaller one, and thought I had robbed him of a whole piece of Jesus. When they returned to their seats, he looked at his mother, disgruntled, and said, "Did you only get half, too?!"

Ask any pastor, and they will tell you story after story about the fun, follies, and wisdom of children in church. At the heart of all of mine sits a young disciple of God who takes his, her, or their faith very seriously while holding it equally lightly. The kids who play and move around antsy next to their parents during much of the service often contribute the most profound insights during the children's sermons. The ones who fidget while they acolyte, leaving other worshippers to doubt their attention on the service, later beautifully explain the purpose, theological, and liturgical significance of each fixture used during communion.

On a certain Sunday, a friend took his daughter to visit a church that did not allow children to take communion. As their family knelt at the rail, the priest passed over my friend's youngest child, merely placing a hand on her head for a quick blessing rather than giving her communion. My friend reported that on the drive home, his daughter complained non-stop about the priest denying her access to the thing that made the service feel holy and meaningful.

While I respect every parent's decision regarding when their child may receive communion, my heart aches when children put their hands forward to take a piece of bread from me, only to see their parents pull the little hands back and shake their heads. Inevitably, the child looks at me questioningly and a little dejected as if to say, "Why does everyone else get this, but I don't?" Those children understand better than many adults the importance of the bread I offer them on God's behalf.

Matthew 18:1-3 reads: "At that time, the disciples came to Jesus and asked, 'Who is the greatest in the kingdom of heaven?' He called a child, whom he put among them, and said, 'Truly I tell you, unless you change and become like children, you will never enter the kingdom of heaven."

Adults mature and lose their playfulness in their faith, sacrificing it on the altar of "reverence" and "solemnity." They often become more concerned with looking the part rather than living it, causing their sincerity to leave along with their playfulness. For many, worship can only look sober and quiet, with no room for exuberance, laughter, or joy. Communion becomes a habit rather than a discipline, and they forget to leave their offerings of sadness, heartache, concern, and heaviness at the rail. They forget too quickly the most basic of lessons: that Jesus loves them and that praising God includes revelry and rowdiness.

One Sunday, one of our chalice bearers came to a young man who attended as a guest of a friend. He watched as his friend and his friend's family dipped their fingers in the chalice full of wine after receiving the bread. This young man popped the bread in his mouth as soon as he received it but then watched as the cup came his way. He had failed to see that the others kept their bread in their hands, choosing not to eat it directly but, instead, dip the little piece of bread in the wine. Not knowing what the others had done when they put their hands in the chalice, the young man dunked his three longer fingers in the wine and wiggled them. He then pulled them out, licked them, and shook them off as he walked away with his host family. The chalice bearer did a magnificent job containing their laughter.

Underneath these stories and others lies a sincere faith and desire to worship wholeheartedly. One minute, children can quietly reflect on the importance of receiving communion, then hold the space lightly enough to stand on the pew and dance during the closing hymn. They find seriousness in their sincere and spirited responses to God.

When did you last play in worship? Or put yourself in the position of not knowing the "right" way to worship but making it up as you went with a heart full of reverence and joy?

I challenge you: Don't make faithfulness and self-reflection a chore.

Let the seriousness with which you approach your faith be that of the youngest disciples. Find joy in your discipline, be ebullient in your praise, and fastidiously festive in your fasting. Take up play in the practice of your faith as a regular discipline. Give God access not only to your solemnity but to your wonder. Don't wait for God in the silence you promise, yet often fail, to set aside for him, but in the din of merry-making as you find your creativity and amazement anew.

For the Sport of It

Yonder is the great and wide sea with its living things too many to number, creatures both small and great. There move the ships, and there is that Leviathan, which you have made for the sport of it.

- Psalm 104:26-27 1979
Episcopal Book of Common Prayer

How often do I scramble to find an answer when my kids ask me "why"? Honestly, every time. If I don't have one, we pull out our phones to ask our favorite search engine to call forth an explanation from the tremendous, semi-reliable online library. Granted, such searches bring up more than the requested answer, fueling fascinating conversations and frequently leaving us with more questions. But the looming "why" still remains.

Why?

We say there must be an answer for everything. In our most helpless and unexplainable moments, our egos grasp the catch-all, yet incredibly unsatisfying and empty phrase: "There must be a reason for everything."

Sadly, we mean by this that God caused everything to happen for a purpose. Reasons explain causality but not purpose, and we crave an affirmation of good intention. Horrible things often happen because someone did something stupid or made a mistake. That empty fact doesn't heal a wound or provide balm. We hunger for a purpose behind it, something to justify the pain.

Though I shared the BCP translation for Psalm 104:26-27 above, I prefer how other translations render the description of the Leviathan:

New International Version: "There the ships go to and fro, and Leviathan, which you formed to frolic there."

New Living Translation: "See the ships sailing along, and Leviathan, which you made to play in the sea."

New American Standard Version: "The ships move along there, And Leviathan, which you have formed to have fun in it."

Aramaic Bible in Plain English: "In it the ships travel, this is Leviathan which you have created to be merry in it."

Dousy-Rheims Bible: "There the ships shall go, This sea dragon which thou hast formed to play therein."

On a recent trip to the beach, I stood in the ocean, so the waves lapped just below my waist. Little minnows schooled around me, flashing their silver sides in the sunlight. Some approached the surface, daring a slight skip above the water before diving again to the safer, darker depths. They grew accustomed to my legs standing among them like the pilings of an oddly shaped pier rooted in the sand. At first, they shied away from my shadow, then took it as permanent and fixed and continued their play around me. Some dared to dart through my legs, avoiding them by inches.

When a bird flew over, casting its quick shadow, the small fish jerked to attention, alert to the danger, before quickly resuming their more relaxed movement once the threat had passed.

We ascribe an evolutionary advantage to every animal behavior, form, color, or movement. We insist on a purpose to everything. Colors serve to camouflage, warn, or attract. Form allows for easier access to food, faster speeds, or amplified hunting prowess. The play of certain species reinforces community norms and structure, thus strengthening bonds that ensure greater survival odds. The silver of the small fish helps them blend with the sunlight flashing off the ripples of the waves, protecting them from overhead hunters.

Yes…yes…I hear that, and the theories are sound. Well done.

But what of the sport of it? I delight in the idea that God creates for the fun of it. What of the purpose of play? What if the reason simply is FUN?

Whales push their enormous bodies hard and fast through the water, breaching the surface to leap into the air, then crash hard on their sides to generate large sprays of water. How is this so different from my brother at fifty years of age, still delighting in running the length of the short diving board to launch his six-foot, one-inch frame in the air, turning just so as he grabs one knee before leaning back to hit the surface at the perfect angle to soak all of those unlucky enough to be sitting at the patio table? I imagine the juvenile whales below the surface exploding into the same giggles as my own children and niece at the sight of an elder doing something purely for fun.

Imagine: What if our automatic answer to "why" became "for the sport of it" instead of "because" followed by a rational, meticulously described purpose? Could it be that our purpose is for fun? Or love? Merriment? Joy? Exuberance?

We spend hours, days, and years searching out the purpose of life, desiring a grandiose answer to justify our experiences and feelings. All along, the answer might be "just because."

Why am I here?

To be merry in it.

What is my purpose?

To play therein.

We like to say God gives us cocreator status in this world. Would we not be better served in this endeavor if we first thought to create for fun? Think of the freedom and joy it would grant us in the creative process!

I watched a pelican dive in front of me to scoop up its meal, carrying a fish away in its gullet. Talons work well for other birds, as do sharp-pointed beaks. Yet look! The pelican crashes headfirst, great mouth open and wings wide, to swallow up its reward, clunky and far from exacting in its execution. Is that not beautiful and fun to behold?

Next time you sit to create, I commend to you this phrase: "For the sport of it" as your great purpose, not perfection or executing a technically excellent performance. Do not set out to write the perfect sentence or paint a museum-worthy scene. Adventure forth, instead, for fun and merriment. Set out for sport.

God knows she did not get every detail perfect when she set the creation of the universe in motion. You may protest this assertion, but she included imperfect humans and other innumerable elements for the pure joy of it. Should we claim our purpose any higher than that of God herself?

"Why, Mama?"

For the sport of it, my child. For the sport of it.

The Prodigal and the Pigs

One day, I stopped by the barn and saw my brother, wearing a terrible scowl, walking beside it.

"What's wrong with you?" I asked.

"I got attacked by a stupid pig!" he shouted in response.

He had grabbed one of the piglets to tag its ear for identification and, apparently, the mama did not take too kindly to his scooping up her baby and came after him. He fussed about wrestling free from her snout as it rooted and poked at him. He shooed her off of him, but not before she charged and got in a good hit, leaving him bruised. He frowned, and then we both laughed about how sore he would be the next day from struggling with an 800-pound angry sow.

In the Christian church, we tell the parable of the Prodigal Son with great regularity because of our affinity for this story of a young man receiving forgiveness from a patient father. Of the story's many interpretations, all end with good news. The story tells that the ne'er-do-well son finds himself among the pigs in a foreign land after losing his fortune, the birthright he demanded from his father. He takes a job tending pigs and grows so hungry that he wishes he could eat their slop. He then realizes it would be better to return home and face his father's disappointment and wrath rather than continue living among the swine.

Though I am no prodigal son, I do relate to this parable. My way of leaving home and gallivanting did not involve claiming an inheritance or turning my back on my family. My sojourn included, instead, serving as a priest in parishes around the Southeast and as a chaplain in schools. I returned home not as a child who lost herself and then returned home to be found. For me, it was simply time to return to my ancestors' land, the birthplace of my grandfather, great-grandfather, and several grandfathers before him.

Before my grandfather had a family, he had a butcher shop. He ran it with two of his brothers and a partner. The rack he used to hold rolls of butcher and wax paper in his shop now hangs on my parents' kitchen wall. Across from it, against their giant hearth, the large bracket of hooks that my grandfather once used to hang meat for drying and displaying to sell now hold baskets of treats for the dog, paper and matches for lighting a fire, decks of cards and games to play with the grandkids, and more.

The building where my grandfather had his shop still stands in my hometown's downtown. Since he closed the doors, it has not been a butcher shop. Instead, in more recent years, others have filled the space with a coffee shop and offices, businesses of some kind or another, a portrait studio for little babies, and now a children's bookstore.

By the time my mother came along, my grandfather had expanded his business to include several farms where he raised cattle and pigs. The most important was the farm of his childhood home, where I live today with my children. He raised my mother on one of his smaller farms in town, keeping plenty of horses and other animals for her to ride and chase. A Walmart Neighborhood grocery store and a Starbucks sit on the property today, ready to serve any number of people who have no idea of the origin of the bacon inside their sous vide egg bites. All the same, they gobble it up with a side of cold brew.

During my sojourning away from the farm, I served parishes in small towns and big cities. When I stepped out of Duke Divinity School into the ministry field, fresh-faced and full of ideas, I embraced my calling to share the good news of God's unfathomable love and to nurture others on their faith journeys. In addition to that good work, I also found myself running vestry meetings, learning best practices for parish bookkeeping, navigating the ins and outs of marketing and advertising, teaching myself desktop publishing for producing newsletters and bulletins, and doing many other things never once mentioned to us in seminary. I occasionally joke that, one day, I'll write a memoir titled "101 Things I Didn't Learn in Seminary."

A particularly enlightening moment during my first year of parish ministry occurred one Saturday afternoon when I learned about septic systems as I mopped up the backflow that oozed over the men's bathroom floor. There is much we don't learn at seminaries— for instance, the activities and responsibilities that suddenly becomes pivotal to a person's work as a minister in God's house are not discussed. Seminary taught me to speak in one vernacular, while parish life introduced me to a wholly different one. Now I have returned home to find myself back with the pigs, learning yet another language devoid of terms like "consubstantiation," "eschatology," and "restricted funds," but full of others such as "erosion mediation," "gilts," and "agritourism."

On a fall day during my first year back home, my brother and I worked with our farm team to prepare a whole hog for a friend's barbecue. We stood next to a 50-gallon drum full of boiling water, watching as one of the workers used our tractor to dip the freshly killed hog into the water to scald its skin. He pulled it out and laid it on a makeshift table where we scraped the thick red bristles from the pig's hide, giving the hog the pink skin everyone thinks of when they picture a pig for roasting. Our grandfather had scars on his legs from when he fell into a scalding vat in one of his slaughtering houses, and I thought of him as I watched the pig lowered in and out of the drum. Our father commented that our grandfather would be proud, were he alive, to see two of his grandchildren taking up the family work, continuing in his line.

For most people, the idea of slopping hogs and tending pigs might make them want to go home, far away from the smells and sounds of the pig pen, the home of their past far removed from the messy job of pig tending. For me, home is precisely there, hearing the hogs snort and grunt as we fill the trough with grain or watch the mamas fling their babies out of their pig pool when it's adult swim time.

I made my sojourn in the world and loved serving God's people. I still work part-time for the church and guest preach, fill in for traveling clergy, or lead workshops and retreats most Saturdays and Sundays. But most of my time is spent on the farm. I gather the scraps from my kitchen as I prepare the meals I love to cook and think of the noises the pigs will make as they gobble them up. From my kitchen sink, I look out the windows of the house my great-grandfather built more than a century and a half ago. In front of me, I see the old horse barn with its thick logs and tin roof. No one remembers who built it, but horses and ponies have called it home for generations, and now my children take their turn, peppermints in hand, to talk with the animals.

After my brother and I laughed about his run-in with the mama pig, I walked into the barn and stepped up to the trough, dropping in those tasty peels from carrots, potatoes, and onions, making a fantastic meal for the hogs. I listened as they snorted and grunted, fussed and moaned, poked and prodded each other. Among that slop and by those pigs, I felt home, down to the bottoms of my soles.

Returning to our roots, wherever they may be and for whatever reason, means finding ourselves and rediscovering the source and core of who we are. I love my vocation as a priest, serving near and far, and have discovered new things about myself everywhere. But nothing speaks to my whole self or helps me discover the totality of who I am nearly as much as returning home.

Prayer in the Kitchen

Three loaves of North Carolina sourdough bread sit on my counter to rise. They have a few hours of rest ahead of them, the natural yeast taking its time to rise and work on the gluten and sugars. I love the deliberateness and wildness of it all, the refusal of the yeast to be tamed and domesticated, preferring to take its time as dictated by the environment rather than by my desires.

Earlier, I mixed the wet dough for some banana bread and now I smell it baking in the oven, counting the minutes until it's done and cooled, ready for me to slice and smear with softened butter. This is true decadence, as I am the only one in the family who eats it. My friend across the road shares my affinity, so I will keep some for myself and then pass the remaining half to him. On the counter sits pasta dough, a project from earlier in the morning, which is also taking its necessary rest. I rolled and abused it to develop it, and now it matures by sleeping on the counter, making itself ready to be put through the literal ringer of the pasta machine.

Sabbath is all around my kitchen. Rest follows work in an unchanging pattern. Work prepares for the sabbath, not the other way around. Rest allows for maturing, developing, progressing, and improving. The kneading, mixing, pressing, and whisking merely prepare the way for the actual "work" that happens when I do nothing but wait and watch.

Sabbath Magic.

My kitchen is my first sanctuary—my place of peace, joy, and wonder. I realize that not everyone shares this sense of peace in the kitchen. Some of you would rather be anywhere but there and find cooking a terrible chore and necessity—as I do whenever I have to iron or clean the bathroom. But the following principles apply wherever you find your sanctuary.

I chose the handle "Prayerful Kitchen" because my kitchen provides my chief place of prayer and meditation.

I do not have specific prayers that I "say" as I cook, no liturgy of the cutlery or litany for soups and stews. I don't pick up a wooden spoon and pray, "Dear Jesus, thank you for this spoon. Thank you for the tree whose wood it comes from, the person (or machine) that made it, and the store that sold it. Amen."

Now that I write that nonexistent prayer, perhaps I should offer it. The whole production chain could use my prayers of thanksgiving and protection, and I could use a moment of grateful pause for the fullness of the work others do to make my meditation possible. But that's a prayer for a different space and time for me. I need the kitchen's silence, even amidst the hum of the mixer or bubble of the pot. Some spaces need to remain unscripted and untamed. Instead, prayer in my kitchen flows unformed and wordless as energy from my chopping, kneading, stirring, and baking.

Most of the time, I play music in the background while I work. The sounds of artists like the Highwomen and Brandi Carlisle resonate deeply in my soul. Hazy, inherited memories from ancestors long since dead float in and out of my awareness as the Wailing Jennies put their spin on the historic music of the mountains. These singers and my forebearers hang out with me in my kitchen, watching over my work and filling me up by pulling me down to my deepest roots. My grandfather rests in his cleaver, which I use to break down chickens into their parts, the same as he did in his butcher shop one hundred years ago. Every woman in my lineage smiles and works through my hands when I pat out biscuits or stew tomatoes. The heavenly hosts of my immediate communion of saints surround me as I pull out a pot or throw potatoes in the sink for washing and peeling. They help prime my mind and heart for the meditation to come.

As I turned the sourdough onto the counter after its first overnight rise, I thought of my daddy and childhood. There was a season when he baked this same bread, and I discovered the recipe online during the COVID lockdown. I remembered the smell it made in the kitchen of my childhood home, lifting up to my bedroom, making me excited for the sweet yeastiness of the first bite. As I kneaded the dough earlier in the day, I rested in those memories and the wonder and freedom of childhood. It was a prayer of thanksgiving for the privilege of having such memories.

Pulling bananas out of the freezer for the quick bread, I thought about my neighbor, who would enjoy most of the loaf to come. I held him in my mind as I mixed the ingredients, mashed the bananas, and folded them into the dough. I raised no specific petitions, thanksgivings, or formulated words; I only held his image there as I worked. God knows what he needs much more than I do. I can hold the space and push positive energy into the world and towards my neighbor.

With one batch of bread rising on the counter and the other in the oven, my spirit was not ready to leave the wide open space of the confines of my kitchen. I sought out the emptiness and holiness of rhythm and action. With plenty of ingredients around, I dumped a mound of flour on the counter and mixed it with some kosher salt. I separated some eggs, allowing the yolks to land in the well I created in the center of the flour, piercing the yolks with my fork to watch the yellow ooze out into the pillowy white. Sliding my fork around the well of yellow potential, I folded in the flour and moved it around, letting my mind relax into the stirring, mixing, and encouraging pattern.

This pattern and prayer filled me with gratitude and joy for my life: my family, the end of the school year, and the blessing of new friends who quickly became family. But I'm also filled with heartache: for friends who move away with the changing of the season, for lost rituals and celebrations, and for friends who hurt due to the changes and chances of this life.

One side of my heart sees everything as perfect with no need for change, while the other sees the holes that it desires more than anything to patch, repair, mend, and make whole.

Those two sides blend together in the meditation of working the egg and flour together so there is no longer the separate bright yellow from the stark white, the slick and slimy from the soft and pillowy. Instead, by pushing and pulling my hands, the two commit to one another into a pale yellow disk, creating something more that will require rest and recovery before continuing to develop into its intended purpose.

My mind stills in the kneading as its two sides face each other to find balance and agreement. One side encourages the other to help where it can and the other to let go where it can't. I look at the sourdough on the counter and think of the work to come with anticipation. The regular flow of work and rest calls my mind to the balance of life, which we too often neglect.

I raise prayers for those I love and those I don't, for the ones I know by name and those wholly unknown to me. I move the eggs and flour until the pale yellow roundness of pasta dough emerges and I push it to the back of the counter, covering it for its rest. I pause for a moment to offer one last prayer: that I might know when my work of preparation has finished and my moment of sabbath has begun. May I never be so caught up in busyness that I neglect the more important work of stillness.

For Rosemary

These are the notes for the sermon I preached a couple of years ago at the funeral of a most beloved friend, Rosemary Wood Dodd. May we all aspire to embrace a mere fraction of the gusto for living that she had . . . and not be afraid of making inevitable mistakes.

Rosemary Dodd relished telling stories, especially ones that may shock listeners. Though not a part of our family by blood, we claimed her forever as one of our more marvelous relations. When Rosemary told her favorite story about our family, her eyes glinted with mischief as she began with the words, "Your Uncle Garland was the first man I ever slept with." Rosemary and Garland arrived into this world only a day apart when our hometown of Gainesville experienced a local baby boom. New mothers and their babies filled the hospital beyond capacity, so the nurses placed Rosemary and Garland in the same bassinet in the nursery.

When we speak at the funeral of a loved one, we become tempted to lionize them and speak to their superhuman qualities. From an early age, we hear that we "shouldn't speak ill of the dead," so we avoid any comments that might be interpreted as unfavorable or detracting from their admirable character. But I know that if I limited my comments to how excellent and perfect Rosemary was, she would stare down at me from heaven, head cocked to the side, mouth drawn down on either side, eyes narrowed, and give me the faintest shake of her head. "Don't you dare…" I can hear her say.

The day before my wedding in 2005, Rosemary hosted my bridesmaids' luncheon at the Piedmont Driving Club in Atlanta. To honor the formal nature of the ladies' luncheon, my wedding party and I decided to wear hats and gloves to the event – make it something special. Of course, that required most of us to go out and buy a hat and search for gloves because not many 21st-century American women keep white gloves and party hats in their wardrobe.

The twelve wedding party members in our hats, gloves, and party dresses piled into a van and made our way to Atlanta. The hesitancy I felt in asking my husbands-to-be's grandmother to hop up into a 15-passenger van only grew as I watched our overly eager driver zoom us into Atlanta. Thanks to the driver's reckless enthusiasm, we arrived early at the club, leaving us at least a half hour to wait in a perfectly appointed lounge while staff members finished preparing our dining room.

With time to kill and a captive audience, Rosemary seized the opportunity to fill us in on her current project of artistic passion: a calendar she would sell to raise money for breast cancer research. A friend had given Rosemary the bust of a woman from mid-thigh to the neck. It had no head but the most wonderfully round belly. Rosemary assumed the model must have been middle-aged, with her sagging breasts and curvy sides. She took the bust as inspiration for a series of twelve paintings, one for each month of the year.

Rosemary gleefully spoke of how she depicted the bust in each month, complete with details on each painting's "nippies and tutus." There we sat, in the Piedmont Driving Club, hats and gloves on, with my mother, my godmother, my fiancé's mother, his godmother, and his grandmother. His grandmother had worn heels and kid gloves when she pushed her infant daughter along the streets of downtown Huntington, WV, in the 1940s. Imagine the look of amusement and apology on my face and that of my mother as we looked from Rosemary to the nervous, giddy expressions of my bridesmaids and the scandalized looks of the older women. Blessedly, my future grandmother-in-law sat serenely smiling, thanks to either her willingness to pretend she did not understand or a failing battery in her hearing aid.

That day, I learned an essential lesson: whereas you or I would say there is a right and a wrong time to share specific stories and information about ourselves, it was never the wrong time to be Rosemary Wood Dodd.

With pleasure and honor, I sat and visited with Rosemary during the last few months of her life. She told me she wanted to talk about my book, *Phe and the Work of Death*, about a death presence who cares for people in their last moments. But soon after my arrival, she wanted, instead, to talk about her life and death. She reflected on what it was like to reach this stage in her life, how it felt to have lost loved ones, recounted lovers and friends from the past, and told more than a few tall tales.

One day, she expressed particular concern over seeing her mom and dad in heaven. Her explanation wandered a bit until she recollected her first memory of ever being in trouble. She couldn't remember her age, only that she was very small. She had found a box of matches in her house and taken them to a quiet corner near a blank wall. She discovered that if she struck the match and blew it out, the end of the stick became a writing utensil. Match after match, she lit and extinguished in order to draw on the blank canvas of the wall. More than eighty years after this discovery, her eyes still shined with faint delight as she shared the tale with me. Obviously, her parents did not feel the same enthusiasm for her discovery. One of her first moments of creating also became her first moment of punishment.

I have difficulty imagining that the brilliant, creative, imaginative

Rosemary experienced reproach for creating some of her first artwork. I experienced her as the grand dame of our town, zealously encouraging and supporting the arts community.

A quiet moment passed between us when she said she worried her parents would scold her upon arriving at heaven. She feared they would view her death as giving up, that her dying occurred in their eyes due to a failure of will. She worried they would tell her she did not fight hard enough or sufficiently strive to push life a little further. As we spoke, we devised a mantra for her, wrote it on a slip of paper, and tacked it to her wall. It read, "I am not giving up. I am going home." With time, her fear lessened, but I cannot confirm it fully disappeared. I hope it did.

When my children were small, someone gave us the book *Beautiful Oops* by Barney Saltzberg. The book's synopsis reads, "It's OK to make a mistake. In fact, hooray for mistakes! A mistake is an adventure in creativity, a portal of discovery. A spill doesn't ruin a drawing—not when it becomes the shape of a goofy animal. And an accidental tear in your paper? Don't be upset about it when you can turn it into the roaring mouth of an alligator."

I love how this story teaches us about self-forgiveness and grace, showing how our mistakes become opportunities for greater creativity, often beyond our initial imaginings.

In the gospels, we find kindred spirits in the bumbling disciples, whose lives bear the marks of many successes and failures. Again and again, they say and do stupid things. Peter, a favorite among them, repeatedly swings from arrogant bravado to withering powerlessness and doubt. We regularly find Jesus shaking his head at Peter because of his eagerness to have the correct answers or actions, followed by his utter lack of understanding and willingness to act. Peter walks on water, then sinks when he remembers he can't. When he sees Jesus at the Transfiguration, he enthusiastically suggests they build three dwellings so Jesus can stay on the mountain forever with Elijah and Moses. Jesus demands to wash the feet of his friends at what becomes the Last Supper, and Peter interrupts with his own demand, "Lord, not only my feet but my hands and my head as well!"

We witness Peter's greatest failing during the passion narrative. Along the way, Jesus tells his disciples that they will all "fall away" and "scatter like sheep." To this, Peter replies, "Even if I must die with you, I will not deny you!" And yet, the cock crows, and Peter devastatingly realizes he has done just that, not once, but three times.

Jesus's disciples became great apostles and leaders not despite their mistakes and doubts but because of them. With every misstep and screw-up, new opportunities opened for them to learn of the depth of God's love. If God cared only about perfection, God would have made sure the authors of scripture left out disciples' failings. Their humanity made them beautiful, complex, and authentic witnesses to the love of God. It is ours that makes us beloved children of God.

As a faithful Daughter of the King, a women's order for prayer and service, Rosemary dutifully wore the cross of the order every day, including her last. The motto of the order states the following:

For His Sake…

I am but one, but I am one.

I cannot do everything, but I can do something.

What I can do, I ought to do.

What I ought to do, by the grace of God I will do.

Lord, what will you have me do?

Rosemary suffered under no illusion that she was perfect. In fact, she loved best telling me of mishaps and missteps. She spoke of mistakes she made as a mother and wife, an artist and daughter, and a member of the fallible human race. But she also knew herself on a most fundamental level to be a marvelous daughter of God.

God hands each of us a blank canvas at birth to do with what we will. As we grow, we stare at it, afraid to make a mark because we don't want to get it wrong. We might spend years studying the craft of painting or drawing, insisting on mastering the art of the single line before we painstakingly add the faintest mark to our blank slate. Meanwhile, people like Rosemary grab the paint and brush and, with abandon, fervidly begin to cover the blank spaces with brilliant color and strokes. Layer upon layer, they add to it, turning one brush stroke into something else and covering this color with that while letting the old color show through. Such artistry means allowing an overloaded brush to drip blue-green streaks down the painting and then turn it into a river filled with trout or mermaids.

To do so is to understand the true meaning of grace. In our baptismal covenant in the Episcopal Church, a creed we repeat several times a year together, the priest asks, "Will you persevere in resisting evil, and, whenever you fall into sin, repent and return to the Lord?" Notice the priest does not ask "if" but "when." The paint will drip, the straight line will go crooked, the path we started on will meander and take us through valleys of shadows of death of our own choosing and making, and all of it is life. Grace is learning not to deny our imperfections but how to turn them into beautiful Ooops!— opportunities to find beauty even in the rain, especially in times when we only would have sun.

I hope, when Rosemary arrived in heaven, some wonderful angel handed her a box of matches, led her to a quiet corner, and gestured at a blank wall. Where she is now, no one will dare take away her matches.

God the Father and Father's Day... It's Complicated.

For many, Father's Day means cookouts and fun gifts for the dad in their lives. Others celebrate father figures and surrogate fathers by calling, Facetiming, or Zooming them. Fathers and fatherly types share stories, laughter, and a hearty dose of nostalgia with those in their care.

But for others, it can be complicated. Not everyone had the fortune of a great biological father, while others miss fathers who have died or disappeared. Some dads face the day after the loss of a child or have estranged kids. Father's Day is not a perfect observance, and it must be noted that it's not joy-filled for all. In fact, it probably includes some level of mixed emotions for most.

The most common criticism for using "Father, Son, and Holy Spirit" in reference to the Trinity is that it is overly male-centric and fails to recognize the sacred feminine, which does have a rich (if somewhat obscured) tradition in Christianity. Given that I'm a female priest, people safely assume that objection resonates with me, and we need to redeem the sacred feminine. I think of God as "Father" and "Mother," generally preferring "Mother" when reflecting on the creative nature of God.

However, for many Christians, the challenge of calling God "Father" shares the same complications as Father's Day. Some of our fellow believers had fathers who failed to show them love, certainly not one to compare to the unconditional love of God. Physical, emotional, and mental abuse at the hands of the head male of a household understandably makes it difficult for someone to connect to God the Father.

For these reasons, early in my seminary studies, I began to prefer other descriptors for the Trinity, such as "Creator, Redeemer, Sustainer." Such alternatives sidestep the complications of referring to God in male-only terms and seem to fix a number of issues. I continue to like this language and use it occasionally in my prayer life and spiritual reflections.

However, I appreciate the argument made by one of my theology professors at Duke to maintain the "Father, Son, and Holy Spirit" monikers. He pointed out that while replacements like "creator, sustainer, redeemer" do solve some issues and can serve an essential purpose, so does the traditional language.

Jesus gave us the title of "Father" for God for a reason; it speaks to the nature of the intimate and caring relationship he recommends we share with God. Jesus took the God known as YHWH by the Jews and brought that God closer, lessening the distance between the divine and the created universe. This God doesn't merely manage or supervise, preferring to sit far away, simply observing with apathy whatever happens.

Christ's use of "Father" shows us God's proper place as someone who loves us – unconditionally in the case of this particular Father – and wants to be a mentor, aid, advisor, and teacher for us. Because of the limits of human language, Jesus had to use ordinary human relationships to come close to describing the nature of the extraordinary one God wishes to share with us.

With all language, "Father" has its limits and imperfections. We don't have the right word for what we mean when we say God, certainly not this kind of God. How can one word encompass the whole of the divine and how we experience it? Whenever we speak of God, we must use metaphor. God the Father helps us come as close as possible, though I encourage others to use "Mother" occasionally. Genesis states "male and female" God created us in the image of the divine, pointing us to the balanced and all-encompassing nature of God's being.

Find the language that best fits your theology and feels comfortable for you. Think of a relationship that had all of these elements: unconditional love, mentorship, advising, teaching, encouraging, challenging, and forgiving. Draw a line from that relationship to God and use whatever language best suits it. Perhaps "Father" or "Mother" fits. Or maybe you find "Teacher" or "Grandparent" or even the name of a particular person more accurately aligns with your experience.

Each of us must find language that resonates and conveys the depth of our unique, individual connection with the divine. No matter our varied experiences with fallible humans, including fathers, we need ways to express our relationship with God that balance specificity with expansiveness and intimacy with vastness.

The Error in Fundamentals

From an early time in our history, Christians sought to return to the roots of the faith. They critiqued the current state of the church in various eras, including our own, by expressing a desire to get back to what Christ originally intended. This is, after all, the determination that drives every fundamentalist movement: How do we recover the fundamentals of the faith and cast off the false ornamentation added by the church over the years?

Jesus taught in parables and through his actions, both beautiful ways of communicating truth but not the most straightforward, concise way of getting his point across. As early as Paul, we have apostles and teachers saying to us, "Well, what Christ really meant was…" in an effort to clarify that which Jesus intentionally kept murky. We hunger for exactness, whereas Christ preferred the indefinite.

What if we err most greatly in wanting to return to some perceived elemental faith in the first place? What if there aren't fundamentals to excavate in the past but truths to discover in the future by forward motion? I fail to believe any Christian or group of Christians understood the full scope of Christ's teachings at any point in the church's history, including those sitting in his presence 2000 years ago. After all, Jesus repeatedly pointed out that his followers lacked understanding and the ability to fully comprehend him.

Why do we keep wanting to go back? Shouldn't our journey be

forward? Paul described the church as the body of Christ – the Christian community as a living, breathing entity that grows and matures, makes mistakes and learns. Why would we want to go back in time if that is the case? I would not put my life today in the hands of 14-year-old me. I loved my younger self, but I know a little more now than I did then. I'd take some of her enthusiasm and passion, definitely some of her energy, and even some of her naivete and innocence. But I wouldn't hand over the keys to the kingdom of my life to her. I wouldn't even trust the mom version of me from five years ago to parent my children now.

Why do some Christians, then, think it a good idea to place our faith of today in the hands of earlier Christians? I don't want a medieval doctor tending to my modern ailments; I'll keep my antibiotics and antiseptics, thank you very much, and leave the bloodletting to history. Our first president died of a throat infection that quickly would have been healed with a round of penicillin or some other such easily obtained and cheap medication of today.

My faith of yesterday had vitality but lacked the depth of the one I enjoy today. My theology and Christology, understanding Christ in his full humanity and divinity, and how the Spirit breathes in my life differ substantially from what I experienced years ago.

The wise prophets of our time add to the story of how Christ moves in the world and do not merely excavate and rework truths from the past. We proclaim belief in the power of the Holy Spirit but deny her sustaining and revelatory power when we tell her she must be wrong in her modern apocalypses. We exhibit a weakness of faith by recommending somehow that her movement today is corrupt in comparison to that which she shared with Christians in previous eras.

I do not want to walk backward with any tradition that entrusts my faith to someone of yesteryear without understanding my modern challenges. Honestly, most of the theologians of history would faint at the sight of female me wearing a collar, to say nothing of their reaction to my being fully vested behind an altar, saying the words of institution.

I can learn from their wisdom and apply it to my life, but I will not limit my understanding solely to their lenses. They did not possess a unique, secret key unlocking the mysteries of the divine that dissolved over time, requiring us to time warp back 100, 200, 1000, or 2000 years to grasp it. Christians falsely believe that should they find the key long lost to time, their faith community would get it "right" this time.

In both Luke's and Matthew's accounts, Jesus encouraged us to "consider the lilies of the field." I doubt the lilies worry much about how their predecessors bloomed four or fifteen seasons ago and whether or not they are doing it correctly according to the lily canon. No. They bloom and shine their faces in the sun, bringing joy to the world in their own time and in their own way.

I read my faith ancestors' works—St. Francis of Assisi and the apostle Paul, great female mystics Hildegard of Bingen and Julian of Norwich, and modern theologians and Biblical scholars Marcus Borg and Walter Brueggemann—with interest and curiosity. Along with Mary Oliver, they have much to teach me. But I also look at my kids' faces, the hummingbirds bickering over the feeder, and the tomorrows that come with as much interest and curiosity. The Spirit is in it all, whispering truths about the divine and all she touches, knowing that I comprehend only the slightest fraction of it all.

Sacrificing Busyness

In preparing a devotion for a meeting one day, I came across a blog post from April 2020 by Amy Hulst on the edify.org site in which she wrestles with the idea of keeping the sabbath amid quarantine and isolation due to COVID. The question before her was how to set aside sabbath time when living in the space of putting everything on hold. It's a worthy read, but this bit in particular caught my attention:

"Sabbath was not only a day to rest, to pause, but it's to be set aside as a sacrifice to the Lord. It's a sacrifice to have no other thing to do, no other place to be, and no other obligation."

Sabbath is the sacrifice of busyness.

Don't skip over that too fast. We may be tempted to think it sounds ridiculous because letting go of some busyness for a time of rest would be easy. We say we would love a "real" day off, with nothing to do and nowhere to go. We say that we wish we weren't so busy. But in reality, people panic when faced with "nothing to do."

Many years ago, my family complained that we were too busy. They spoke truthfully; I have a terrible habit of overscheduling all of us, even during our time off. I like to fill our calendar with outings and experiences out of a case of FOMO (fear of missing out). The mom in me also wants to ensure I'm being a good parent by exposing my kids to ALL THE THINGS.

I responded to their pleas by running an experiment. I blocked off several weekends on our calendar and intentionally did not plan a single activity. I left the weekends open for a whole lot of nothingness. If people invited us to join their activities or if I saw a local event advertised, I politely declined or ignored the ad, resisting the urge to add anything to our schedule to honor the family's desire and need for time away from everything.

I waited for my family's reaction, and they did not surprise me. By noon on Saturday, one (or all) of them would ask if we had plans that evening or for Sunday. When I answered "No," they asked if we could call another family or friends to come over or go out and do something. They could stand the nothingness from Friday after school to noon on Saturday, but no longer. I could easily blame this on the fact that all five of us are extroverts, and that wouldn't be wrong, but I also found it very telling.

I find it challenging to sit still and do nothing without feeling guilt nesting in my mind. Even as I sit and write this, the little mouse runs on its wheel in the back of my brain, shouting out the list of things I should be doing instead. It tells me I must be more productive because it cannot bear to think of writing as fruitful. Writing serves me, whereas getting up and doing something would serve others. Therefore, writing seems selfish.

Sacrificing busyness.

Are we not called to sacrifice the idols of our life on the altar of God? God commands us to bust them apart and let them go, with the admission that we set them above God in the daily machinations of our lives.

Is busyness not the biggest idol of them all?

We learn early that our worth resides in our busyness. We can gauge the shape of our own being only when it moves in some act of productivity. Pride wells inside us when we "lament" (read: brag) about how overworked, overloaded, and busy we are.

Busyness glows as a green hologram floating high above the altar on which we lay our lives, sacrificing ourselves in hopes we may appease the false god of worth and value.

We struggle to admit the power and control lie in our hands to make a change, to stand and wrestle out of its hiding place whichever projector we allow to cast that idol of busyness before us. Sabbath opens the permission and will to smash and destroy the illusion that this busyness somehow brings us purpose or success.

Sacrifice requires effort and heartache, giving up something to the point of hurting. We don't easily sacrifice any worthy offering we lift up. Sacrifice demands hardship, and sacrificing busyness might be the most significant hardship we could face.

Think of how difficult you might find it to do nothing. I underwent physical therapy for an injury this past year, and one day, my therapist told me about his "nothing box," a mental place he goes to think of nothing. I could not conceive of this. I struggle to recall a time when I had nothing racing through my mind - no thought, no voice, no image, no to-do list, no sense of guilt or shame for standing still. The idea of a nothing box felt like an unobtainable dream, one for which I long yet doubt I could find. Even on days when I take medication for my ADHD, the voices grow quieter but do not disappear.

Finding a day for nothing does not include filling the void by binge-watching a favorite show. We rationalize time set aside for bubble baths or three seasons of the latest "guilty pleasure" on our favorite streaming service by calling it "self-care," thus making it "productive" time because we gave it a purpose. We even assign our rest time a job of some sort.

Sabbath is sacrificing busyness.

Authentically and honestly, consider what this sacrifice means for you. Can you bear not to grasp for validation in what you do but instead rest quietly in the affirmation that comes with the simple, God-given command to "keep the sabbath holy?" We find it nearly impossible to believe God calls us "beloved" simply for our being and not for our doing.

Busyness is a difficult drug to quit. I like feeling I matter and have value because of the life God granted me, but our world tells me and you that we have little to no value outside of our capacity to produce. I have yet to figure out the magic mantra that releases me from the hold of this idol.

God begs us for time and quiet, stillness in our lives through which we feel more strongly our connection with the divine. God asks only one-seventh of our time, so small compared to the abundance God showers on us, during which he restores us and reminds us of the true nature of our being. We choose whether or not to accept his invitation, to set aside our idol and its false promise of worthiness instead of stepping into the presence of the one who looked at us from the first day we breathed life and loved us, declaring us more than enough, just as we are.

Homemade Butter and the Drip, Dripping of Sabbath Time

A steady drip rings out in my kitchen, and I listen to the singing of the metal bowl, which catches every drop. Usually, I detest repetitive sounds—the ticking of a clock, the smacking of chewing gum, the clicking of a ballpoint pen. But this sound is different. Each drop pops through the surface of the buttermilk that has already been collected below. Instead of creating an annoyance, this sound calms my mind and my soul. I decided to make homemade cultured butter in preparation for an upcoming tea and, later, a luncheon. Now, I find myself at the most challenging moment of the process: waiting for the buttermilk to drain off the butter.

Our modern age of food processors makes for easy butter making. The machine does the difficult work of "churning" in mere seconds which, in times past, working hands took half an hour or more to accomplish. I use one part cultured buttermilk to four parts heavy cream, mixing the two kinds of milk together, then leaving them to sit uncovered for 18-24 hours in my microwave. After the cultures work their magic on the cream, all of it goes into the Cuisinart for a quick whirr. I listen to the spinning liquid as the cream thickens, making the machine's motor work harder. Then, as the fats break apart from the liquid, the sound changes from straining to sloshing. I dump the floating bits of milk fat with their surrounding liquid into a tea towel (which I prefer to cheesecloth) that lies inside our large colander with a bowl underneath. I tie up the ends of the cloth to make a tidy pouch secured with the ever-trusty rubber band. The parcel then hangs from a knob on one of my upper kitchen cabinets above a waiting metal bowl.

I now wait and listen to the buttermilk drip. Later, I'll dump the butter out of its package and into a clean bowl to continue kneading the buttermilk out of the butter, dumping it in the bowl with the rest. Beautiful, fresh yellow butter forms a ball to which I'll add some salt, then, in my impatience, smear some of the fresh creamy goodness on a piece of toast or freshly baked scone before putting the rest in the fridge to harden.

But first is the waiting, a discipline for which I have little talent. I have plenty of patience for others but nearly none for myself or inanimate objects. I find it excruciating to wait for gravity and physics to work on the butter and buttermilk. Surprisingly, the dripping doesn't exacerbate my impatience but settles me instead. It sings out to me as a call to pay attention.

One of the reasons I love to cook as much as I do is because it is the work of preparation. Peeling, chopping, searing, baking, sauteing, I do it all happily in service of a future moment when I, with my friends and family, get to sit and relax around a table. We will pass around the warm scones and fresh butter, settling into our chairs to chat, laugh, and share. I invest my time in the kitchen because I know it will yield great rewards once we sit together.

As I listen to the buttermilk dripping, my mind calls my attention to our observant Jewish brothers and sisters who keep a strict sabbath, one in which they do not work, including turning on or off stoves or even lights. Instead, the family will gather to reflect and be still for the day. You can't settle into a day of no work without making significant preparations. The house and the food must be ready to require no work from family members on the sabbath, allowing them to take a full day of rest.

When was the last time you observed a full day of sabbath? For those of us who rarely, if ever, do so, we enter into rare sabbath days extremely ill-prepared. We do not know how to plan sufficiently to ensure an uninterrupted time of reflection and restoration. Whenever I think I have positioned myself well for a "day off," I wake to a long list of "to-dos" that I feel necessary to complete before fully relaxing. How long will that list take? Two hours? Three? Half of my sabbath disappears because of my lack of preparation.

I hear the singing of the buttermilk again as it drops into the bowl below. I know sabbath-keeping is worth every moment of preparation it requires. If I didn't, I wouldn't be hanging out in my kitchen, waiting for liquid to drain off butter, a product I could have bought cheaply at the grocery store.

I chide myself in this moment. I have not tended well to my sabbath-keeping, much less in my preparations. It takes intentionality to set aside times of rest to sit in the presence of God, and I have been remiss in my own arrangements.

How about you? A day off is different from a day spent in keeping sabbath time. When was the last time you fully prepared for and lived into sabbath rest?

Over my years of cooking, I have learned to turn the kitchen rhythms into smaller moments of sabbath keeping. A morning spent baking bread becomes quiet hours conversing with God about my concerns, fears, hopes, and desires. I have yet to succeed in full sabbath days, but these small moments, like listening to a bowl sing with the dripping of buttermilk, grant me more manageable windows for re-creation. Perhaps, as my children grow and head off to college, I might find 24-hour stretches of time for sabbath growth. In the meantime, I'll remain happy with floured hands, dirty dishes, and the meditative motions of the kitchen that open my attention to feel the Spirit's movements in my heart.

Faith in Stitches

A depiction of Mary and Child hangs on the wall of my kitchen. A self-taught fabric artist hailing from Mississippi fashioned this Madonna and Infant Jesus out of swaths of fabric, a thousand buttons, and millions of tiny stitches made by her hand. A friend and his wife purchased it years ago at a folk art show in Atlanta, then generously made a gift of it to me when they downsized.

It is a piece to feast on with your fingers as much as your eyes. A wealth of textures combines to create the artist's vision of Jesus and his mother. The artist employed velvet, woven carpet, heavily embroidered material, lace, and more. Buttons, woven ribbons, and beads contribute to the immense detail work that makes the tapestry an icon rather than a mundane portrait.

The image perfectly portrays the artist's unique, lived faith. Each bead and button represents a moment in the artist's life; each one holds the memory of a time she encountered God. A piece of lace might have come from a wedding gown that reminded her of Christ's love for his church or maybe for the miracle of being chosen and loved. Perhaps a swatch of pink belonged to a stuffed elephant once held by a child at her grandmother's funeral, forever memorializing the child's first encounter with death and the hope of Resurrection. Perhaps the artist, as she picked daffodils one spring afternoon, heard God call her name and reminded her of her worth, the daffodils then inspiring the fabric she chose for Mary's halo.

Our faith does not begin with belief. It starts with questions and continues with encounters. Faith grows with prayer and during times of crisis, blooming in moments of inexpressible joy. With every encounter with the divine, we pick up buttons and collect tiny scraps of fabric. Larger pieces mark our battles with illness and others from the loss of a loved one. Particularly shiny beads we put in our pockets as they sparkle like the water at our child's baptism. When we watched the woman in front of us buy another stranger coffee because she saw how cold shook the stranger's body, we found a brown button and tossed it in our jacket pocket.

Now and again, we stop long enough to pull out our collected trinkets, doodads, and baubles. We turn each over in our minds, remembering the moments from which they came. Then, we take needle and thread in hand to lovingly stitch each into the tapestry of our hearts, the one that tells the story of our relationship with the divine.

To children, this tapestry may look more like a malformed rainbow, an explosion of joyful, pure, transparent color. The natural heartbreak of life adds splashes of grey or deep blues, maybe a swath of black now and again. The embellishments become more varied in size and texture. Some catch us by surprise. We don't remember picking up a piece of God in that particular moment of crushing pain. Still, there it is, woven into the tapestry as clearly and essentially as the piece lovingly collected at the peak of our joy.

Over time, we step back occasionally, pulling our attention away from the details in order to take in the whole, and in those moments, we see a beautiful, imperfect image of God. The artist of my Mary and Child gave them the pinkest skin and blondest hair, their cheeks like those of toy soldiers at Christmas. In her vision, Jesus has little fingers resembling small pink grape clusters. Nonetheless, Mary and Child are there, as clear as day; the artist perfectly captured God in the imperfection of her vision of a life lived in faith.

No one can tell us precisely what God looks like or how God thinks. No one can tell us if God is a he, a she, or if she likes peanut butter and jelly sandwiches and favors people with red hair. None of us can be sure about much when it comes to God. What we can do is share the tapestries of our lives, the painstaking stitches made by our own hands, and the bits and baubles we have collected over the years. Each of our icons is perfect in its imperfections. They are beautiful, as surely as is each one of us.

We need to look upon our tapestries, our malformed images of God, and call them "Good," for God did the same for us the day she stepped back and marveled at her creation.

Jesus Wept, So Why Can't We?

One day, I sat with a friend as she spoke of a recent loss in her life. Tears began falling as she shared her heartbreak, but then stopped to apologize for crying. She had experienced a profound loss and yet, she felt ashamed by the tears naturally flowing from her emotions. Too often I have repeated this scene with friends, family, and church members alike.

I'm not sure where we get the idea that crying shows weakness or how we manage to heap shame on loss by reprimanding ourselves or others when the tears fall. God gave us the ability to cry for a purpose; it is not a mistake God made in our creation. After I sat with my friend, I sat in the quiet of my room and the following reflection poured forth.

"Jesus wept." The shortest passage in the bible is John 11:35.

Jesus wept because he heard of the death of Lazarus, a man he knew and loved, a friend who was like family.

Jesus wept out of love and grief, not out of doubt.

Jesus wept because he had a human heart, and humans respond to loss and sadness with tears and runny noses.

Jesus wept because it is what anyone with a heart does when unwelcome news damages and breaks it.

Jesus wept, but the world didn't stop. No one judged him. No one left him.

Jesus wept, and no one questioned whether he was fit to lead or fit to serve.

Jesus wept in front of his followers, in a public place for all to see, and no one turned away, no one tried to hide him, no one tried to quiet him.

Jesus wept without shame or embarrassment because weeping is as much a part of human life as laughter.

Jesus wept because tears are prayers of thanksgiving in the depths of sorrow. Each tear lifts praise for a life lived that now is gone, gratitude for a gift given that is no more, but we loved while we had it, a gift so great that the absence of it pains us to our very core.

Jesus wept because we celebrate life with smiles, joy, heartbreak, and sorrow.

Jesus wept because he loved, and loving risks it all for the sake of the other. Loving pushes your heart to swell and break because that's how God created each one of us.

Jesus wept because the pain of love is as rewarding and vital as the elation of ecstasy.

Jesus wept for himself and his friends but not out of selfishness or doubt. We can mourn the loss in the same moment we have deep and abiding faith that death doesn't have the last word.

Jesus wept because faith does not ask for 24/7 smiles and praise but steadfastness in the face of loss and pain.

Jesus wept because he could, in a full embrace of his humanity and capacity for life— love, suffering, loss, joy, elation, and friendship.

Jesus wept because he should—because that's what we do when someone we love leaves us, sometimes even when we know it won't last forever.

Jesus wept, showing us yet another stone in the path that paves the way of life, the way of the cross, the way of faith, the way of discipleship and dedication to following him.

Jesus wept, so why can't we? Why don't we? Are we less human? Do we feel love and loss any less? Do we think ourselves better or more robust than the almighty? Must we feel ashamed and embarrassed by our tears, when God himself cried openly and with abandon?

Jesus wept. And so do we, can we, should we.

Gratitude in Offering

A new king comes to power and immediately announces he has abolished the old taxation system. The subjects wait with great anxiety to hear what will replace the system they have known. Past kings demanded their subjects pay different percentages of their yearly income and harvests. The people of the kingdom know punishment awaits anyone who fails to comply with the king's orders. Not knowing the expectations of the new king causes great consternation and gnashing of teeth across the kingdom.

The traditional day of taxation arrives, but the new king has yet to announce his demands. The people line up outside the castle with goods representing the ten percent tax rate required by the previous ruler. They wait and wait for the gates to open and for the king to step forward, but nothing happens. After a full day of standing in line, the people become restless and even more worried. Finally, the king looks down from a balcony on the side of the castle and repeats that he has abolished the old taxation system. But people stay where they stand, waiting to hear the king detail a new taxation system to replace the old one, likely including a increase the former rate, and what day they will be expected to render such taxes. Instead, the king waves and tells them all to go home and back to their fields, and then he turns and walks back into the castle.

Over the next several months, the king walks through the kingdom and visits his subjects in their fields and homes, unlike any king who came before him. Kings do not spend time with their subjects and certainly do not visit them in the fields where they work. The people assume the king comes among them to see for himself how much they harvest or how much they make. The king may only trust his subjects to give him part of the demanded tax. If he walks among them, he will better understand how much his people will owe him to guard against the subjects' paying less than their assessed amount.

The king's presence among them makes the people nervous and resentful, so they begin to inquire about the king's desires and purpose in visiting with them in their fields. The king says he is interested in their hard work and inquires about how they find fulfillment in their work. He wants to know their families and understand how he might better serve them as their ruler. He cares about his subjects and wants to provide for them in the best way possible.

Out of utter confusion and frustration, the subjects continue to fill the void of demands and expectations by coming up with their own. They tell one another stories of inevitable terrible punishments if they do not pay the king enormous sums of money and harvest yields as tributes to him. They spread rumors that the king plans to build a massive dungeon under the castle where subjects will be thrown for decades if they fail to pay him 40, 50, 60, or even 90% of their harvest.

Once again, the subjects line up outside the castle on their customary tax day, this time with even more extensive prepared offerings. They grumble and complain that the king would demand so much of them—even their entire livelihood. They fuss as they wait for the king to appear to take their taxes or throw them in the dungeon for failure of payment. The citizens, tired of waiting, look at one another, compare their offerings, and worry that they might not have brought enough because their neighbor brought twice as much. They begin to bicker and argue among themselves.

Once again, the king comes out on the balcony, reminds them of his previous announcement, and tries to send them home. But many of his subjects stay where they stand. The following day, he finds that several have chained themselves to the castle's walls. A few of them told the rest that they had angered the king because they did not bring enough on tax day, so he sent them away. These leaders have convinced people that the king will soon come to enslave them for their failures, and they can only gain favor and some forgiveness by chaining themselves before the king does. He will show mercy on them for showing their wretchedness and locking themselves up.

The king comes out, breaks the chains, and sends them home again.

The following year, the people show up at the castle's doors on tax day. This time, some have brought 1%, some 6%, and others as much as 50% of their year's earnings. No one grumbles or judges their offering against their neighbor's. The king steps out on the balcony to ask why they have come since they are no longer bound to any tax system. The people tell him they have not brought taxes but offerings of thanksgiving.

The day after he walked into their fields with them, he had supplies sent to address the specific needs of each of his subjects. If a farmer had a broken fence, he sent others to help with fresh fencing supplies. If a family lost their livelihood because their milk cow was killed by a wolf, he sent another. The people have come to show their gratitude for the king's faithfulness to them, not because they have to, but because they want to. Life now is infinitely better than ever before, and they want the king to understand how thankful they are for his generosity, care, and kindness.

The king does not judge their gifts, assessing them for adequacy or generosity. Instead, he accepts their offerings, acknowledging each one as sufficient. Before he brings the goods into the castle storerooms, he asks his subjects to consider who in the kingdom might need their offerings. If they know someone who could benefit from what they have, he tells them to take their offering to their neighbor first and then bring it to him. The king only wants what remains to store and use when he sees a needy subject.

I imagine this to be God's experience in watching humanity. Patiently, God watches as we try to twist and redefine grace, unable to accept it as unbounded and infinite. We expect a particular economy that demands tit-for-tat based on bartering and exchange. We try to make God live by human rules of commerce, by telling ourselves and one another that we must earn God's grace and love or that, having received it, we now owe a crushing debt to God.

God desires a response from our hearts of gratitude and love, but we try to make our offering compulsory. We cannot believe God loves us unconditionally enough to pour her grace upon us with abundance. We make new rules and spread misconceptions because we cannot accept such an immense gift. Meanwhile, God waits and watches, wanting us not on our knees but with arms open, ready and willing to return even a tiny fraction of the love she already has given.

Living in such love and grace is true freedom. If God required specific offerings or demanded certain acts of contrition, we would feel ourselves bound in chains. The minute something becomes compulsory, we lose our freedom. But a gift, an offering, an act of love can only be given if it comes voluntarily and from the heart out of a pure desire to show appreciation.

The kingdom of God will be made real the day we allow ourselves and one another freedom, the day we bring our offerings out of unbounded thanksgiving and love.

Consider the Dandelion

It seems every ad for weed killers targets the much-maligned and humble dandelion. The threatening, deep voiceover lists the many threats to a pristine lawn as the camera zooms in on a healthy dandelion with a bright yellow flower. A hand appears from the side of the screen to grab the bottle of weed killer and, with sniper precision, trains the spray on the dandelion and pulls the trigger. A time-lapse of the plant shows the flower starting to droop, followed by the yellowing and browning of the leaves until the entire plant goes from regal and crowned to shriveled and decrepit. Trumpets blast as the happy lawn owner vanquishes the enemy. His lawn is safe once again!

I have an affinity for dandelions and fruitlessly root for the underdog in these commercials. Dandelions are incredible plants. We can use the leaves to make a traditional salad. The bright yellow flowers smell of sunshine, making them delightful flavorings for cookies and fermenting wine. For centuries, healers collected them for their medicinal properties.

But their heads, once the bloom fades and the fluffy seeds arrive, have the magical ability to grant wishes! I remember lying in the grass, plucking the dandelions and blowing to watch the seeds take flight on the wind of my breath. My friends and I would race from one pristine seed head to another, wanting to be the first to reach the plant and gain the wish. But we had to be careful and not run full-stop to the white puffball; otherwise, the wind from our legs might cause some of the seeds to release early and take flight. This would ruin the wish because, as everyone knows, only a perfectly intact and fully developed seed head could grant wishes. We would snatch up the fluffy orb, close our eyes, make a wish, and gently blow on the former flower to watch the seeds fly away, carrying our wish to the magical powers that be.

Those seeds might be the real miracle of the plant, tenacious in their determination to root in any condition. They flourish in the rich soil of a well-tended lawn but, equally, find a home in the cracks of a paved driveway or the slightest collection of soil in the crag of a rock. World be damned, they are going to grow into the plant God intended. For this very reason, dandelions frustrate the most patient of gardeners.

Imagine if we considered these seeds precious and painstakingly saved them, gingerly placing them in small glass boxes rimmed in gold to hang them from chains around our necks. When we traveled to see family, we would take dandelion seeds enshrined in plastic with poems to give as gifts.

This gives us some sense of what it was like for those who heard Jesus compare the kingdom of God to a mustard seed. Like many things in the Bible, our distance in time and space from Christ has allowed us to domesticate the radical wildness of this parable. Tiny mustard seeds are light enough to be carried by the wind and grow everywhere with determination and vigor. Their seeds and leaves have medicinal properties, and people use them in cooking. For this reason, we can consider them the dandelions of Christ's time, and it must have sounded ludicrous for Jesus to compare something as mysterious and precious as the kingdom of God to the most mundane of plants.

The kingdom of God is like a dandelion seed. The seed takes flight at the slightest whisper of wind from the Holy Spirit. It floats until it finds a meager amount of soil, where it will take root and grow, even against all odds. It has the tenacious ability to dig into the darkest and coldest of hearts to bring healing and light.

It grows to our consternation at times. We look at a seemingly barren landscape and think, "No. The kingdom of heaven can't be in this place, among these people." And yet, the Spirit is there, growing in hearts, between the cracks. We look at someone we consider depraved, a heartless enemy, and yet, God's love grows inside of them, having carried a seed on the breath of the Spirit and encouraged it to spread roots.

If we adults remembered to be more like the children, we would run, rush, or even snatch up the next seed head to make a wish and blow, spreading kingdom seeds as far as our breath could carry. We spend too much time judging which people and places might have the kingdom within them, including which ones might be worthy for God to receive and call his own. Instead, we should be in the business of wonder, wishes, and excitement as we whisper to the Spirit, "Take flight!" and watch the seeds go, not where we design or desire, but where God would carry them out of his abundant grace and love.

The kingdom of God knows no boundaries, no more than a dandelion seed knows fences and property lines. As Christians, the Spirit calls us into this world, one littered with kingdom seeds that could use our encouragement and watering, including those deep within our own hearts.

Standing in My Sun

On a beautiful and warm sunny September Sunday, I greeted churchgoers on the patio of the parish I had joined that morning as their newest seminary student. I took to the congregation quickly with the eagerness of a seminarian's naïveté. The parishioners welcomed me with easy smiles, understanding better than I the role they would play in my formation as a priest. In my arrogant enthusiasm, I saw a church full of members to whom I would be a pastor for the first time, and I was not aware of the many ways they would pastor me.

The church doors opened onto a small courtyard of dark red bricks surrounded by curved walls. The members and clergy gathered every Sunday in this semicircular space to enjoy cookies and lemonade and visit after the later service. I stood on the far side of the courtyard against the low wall, smiling happily to members as they greeted the rector, associate rector and, finally me, their newest seminarian. The brick underfoot felt solid, a firm foundation for me on my nervous but happy first day. I felt good about the morning and how I handled myself during the get-to-know-you forum between the services. I did not know that the ground beneath my feet and the rigid walls enclosing it would soon become a trap.

Amidst the cheerful faces, I spotted one wearing a frown of dogged determination. A woman in her early sixties focused all of her attention on me and forged a direct path to come to stand before me. I am still unsure how she made that walk so quickly through the thick crowd filling the patio. She marched at me, not with an outstretched hand but a pointing finger.

It took me a moment to realize that she considered herself in a position of authority that lent her the right to reprimand me. Why? I had just begun my tenure with this parish that day. My only responsibility in the service and all morning was to be present and seen. I knew well enough that I could have done nothing to offend but, still, I found myself before a highly displeased member.

The next fifteen minutes felt to me like an eternity as the woman forced me to listen to her prepared monologue. "Women should not be priests," she declared, then proceeded to enumerate the myriad reasons why I was an apostate and an offense. My feet didn't move an inch, but it felt like she backed me against the courtyard wall, her commanding stance absorbing every ray of light out of the sky. The world narrowed to the space between the tip of my nose and the tip of hers - mine pointed down as she was shorter than I was, and hers twisted upwards in a sneer that distorted her face.

I shuddered as if her rage brewed a sudden storm, consuming all the light and warmth from the September sky. The sun seemed to fade as she trapped me in her shadow until her diatribe ceased.

After the first few minutes, I stopped listening to her old and tired arguments, which others before her have repeated over millennia. After all, I am a Southern woman called to the man's world of church leadership. That morning, I faced the unexpected challenge of the person before me demanding a response to all the usual arguments. She carried herself in a way that implicitly conveyed the question, "What do you have to say for yourself, young lady?" What should I say to this person who would breathe into herself every dream and aspiration for the ministry I had so that she may consume and end it?

She doggedly addressed me with the hope that her speech would bring about the clanging echo of a closing door that would cut off my ill-conceived future and the possibility that she and I would relate in any way as parishioner and priest. As she droned on, I began to hear not a slamming door but the sound waves of light, my sun. A crack opened past the darkness of her imposing body so that the light streamed onto my face and, with it, the Spirit. I heard a voice pronounce the words that became an anchor for me in this storm and others to come: "I called you. She didn't." Without an ounce of doubt, I knew they came from God as a push for me to stand tall. Those words gave me the strength to stand, my face toward the coming sun, and finish listening with a smile and a boost of patience.

She finally paused, a look of expectation and triumph on her face. I realized she had finished, and I breathed in deeply the warm, sunny September Sunday breeze. The eclipse had passed, and I remained unmoved in the sun's path to bathe in it once again.

With what can only be the Spirit's inspiration, I smiled, then shook the hand that had been pointing its finger in my face only moments before. I looked her in the eyes and said, "Thank you for sharing with me. I look forward to seeing you every week."

We hadn't moved from our little corner of the courtyard, but my whole world had shifted. From that moment on, I knew that no one could stand between me and the sun, no matter how hard they tried.

My response stunned her, and she stood in silence for a moment. Whatever she may have expected, that was not it. She said nothing and wandered off. She did not speak another word to me in the two years I served that parish. She and her husband would come through the greeting line after the service; he would shake my hand, but she would only look at me incredulously.

My moment of victory came during Advent of my second year as the parish's seminarian. My would-be nemesis liked to sit near the front of the church where she could see our rector, whom she adored. She told me that September morning that he was the only reason they attended our church. I had grown accustomed to seeing her on the second pew, eyes trained on him as he preached, a recorder in her hand so she may enjoy his words again later. I preached my third sermon on that victorious December morning, and as I looked up from my manuscript, I caught her eye briefly before she turned away. Despite her effort to escape my attention, I could not miss the recorder in her hand, lifted from her elbow where it rested on her knee, high enough to catch every word I spoke.

Enzymes and Hospitality

I am a bit of a science nerd. I do not claim to be overly knowledgeable or a regular reader of scientific books. Still, I love watching biological processes at work and observing how the laws of physics govern our world.

I remember learning about enzymes in high school, and my love and fascination for them have not faded. As catalysts, enzymes expedite chemical reactions. When atoms combine to form new molecules, enzymes often do the heavy work to bring them together. The enzymes do not become a part of the new molecule but connect the essential elements and make them happier. Nature provides a facilitator to speed up processes and bring into contact things that otherwise may not have bumped against each other.

Enzymes create an active site for two substrates to connect. The enzyme brings these substrates together until they meld into a new product. It then releases from the enzyme, allowing the enzyme to reset its active site and prepare for new substrates. Amazing!

When we engage in the ministry of hospitality, I believe we do the work of an enzyme. We set a table, clean up our lawn, arrange plates and napkins, and prepare food. In essence, we make ready our active site. Then our guests, our substrates, arrive. Some guests know each other already and share a bond, but others will meet for the first time. They will introduce themselves, get to know each other, forming a new bond. By the time they leave, these substrates will have a relationship with one another, and we, the hosts and catalysts, can clean and reset the active site for another meeting.

I watched this process in action when a large group gathered at my house to celebrate my son's birthday and mark Oktoberfest. People from four different parts of our lives attended, many having never met. Once our guests arrived, I served dinner and walked around to watch and listen. On the deck, a family new to the area visited with families from various local school communities and members of our church. On the lawn, the parent of a new kindergartener visited with the fifth-grade teacher from her child's school. The parent called me over and said, "My new BFF!" wrapping her arm around the teacher. "We had the same nickname growing up! We're just finding out what else we have in common."

The following day, I saw on Facebook that these two women had commented on each other's posts and shared a recipe. Another friend of mine of fifteen years commented on the feed of someone else I had known twenty-two years ago. The two people live in different parts of the country and would not know each other if it were not for attending an event at my house years before. Now, they are friends.

Enzymatic activity at work.

I feel the same work in action when I serve in my capacity as a priest, especially around the altar. So much of my job has included connecting people so that ministry grows out of their new relationship organically and dynamically. I hear when someone shares an interest that matches another person's resources, and I work to bring them together to talk, to see if a new product might result from our efforts. Similarly, I set the table on Sunday morning for the congregation to be fed by God. The gathering of people around the altar creates a new product: the body of Christ. I am not the host, simply the catalyst, and I love this work.

Hospitality built the early church with followers of the burgeoning Christian movement welcoming apostles into their homes for respite. Paul and his companions accepted Lydia's offer to stay with her, after converting her and her household. We regard her as the first documented Christian convert in Europe and her home became a refuge and a base of operations for Paul during his stay.

I sometimes hear people disparage their capacity and gift, or lack thereof, for hospitality. Some say they can't host people to their houses because their homes aren't perfect and can't create the "perfect" environment. Similarly, people will criticize someone for hosting parties to "show off" their fashionable houses and expert ability to pull off a gathering.

In sharing these thoughts, we discourage one another from performing one of the most fundamental ministries. Welcoming each other through acts of hospitality is a primary ministry that gives birth to many more. I don't delight in having people in my home because I get to show it off. On the contrary, I exert no extra effort to make everything look perfect or tidy. I prefer seeing people meet, laugh, connect, eat well, and leave happier than when they came and with new bonds and relationships. That happens best when guests relax, unafraid of messing up a pristine setting or dirtying starched linens.

In an age of isolation and alienation, we need more enzymes working as catalysts to bring people together. We hunger for connection, relationship, renewal, and purpose, but this only happens if we first get people together. Consider ways you serve as a catalyst in your community and your role in making connections and strengthening relationships. You may find more opportunities to bring unlikely friends together.

I grow weary of the divisions in the world around me. News outlets and political interest groups benefit from polarizing people and distancing their audiences from others. Our obsession with in-or-out mentalities grows to the extent that we cease to be "friends" online, to say nothing of in person.

We cannot cure hatred alone, but we can provide a balm to a hurting world by engaging in enzymatic activity. For now, we may need ground rules for guests, like setting politics aside until after whatever upcoming election has elevated our ire. Though I like a good political debate, truthfully, these days, I prefer to chat about a new favorite cheese or hear someone talk about their cat's latest antics.

When I come to your house, I promise to relax into your enzymatic work, seeking out connections with other guests previously unknown to me, and give thanks for your planning and thoughtfulness. When you come, I won't spend days making my home spotless, but I will have plenty of food and interesting people for you to meet. Slowly, through both of our efforts, we can bring together that which otherwise would be kept apart.

Hope in the Face of a Ring Bearer

Many summers ago, I had the honor of preaching at the wedding of two women on the banks of a lake in Knoxville, TN. The couple, skilled at organizing, planned way ahead. They asked me more than a year and a half before the event if I would participate in their big celebration. Thrilled at the news of their engagement, I put the wedding date on my calendar and looked forward to being in Knoxville with them.

I drove to Tennessee the weekend of the wedding, full of excitement, and located the venue: a beautiful barn explicitly built for significant events and boasting lake views. Walking around to enjoy the views, I bumped into the other priest who would preside over the nuptials. We greeted each other with the usual questions of, "Where did you go to seminary?" and, "Do you know (this or that other priest)?" Within short order, the wedding planner connected with us, and we found her great to work with, which isn't always the case for clergy.

The other priest and I walked down to the ceremony site, located below the event barn, right on the banks of the lake. Thankfully, trees canopy the area from the summer sun, keeping us cool as we waited for the planner to organize the wedding party and send them our way. The bridesmaids and "best buds" found their places on either side of us, and we watched the two brides enter on either arm of their daughter. Love seemed to become a mother hen, fluffing us under her wings and settling over us all. The smiles of the brides infected all of us present as we listened for instructions from the planner and the other priest.

My colleague walked the wedding party through the ceremony, reaching the point where the ring bearer should step forward to hand over the rings. Of course, the maid of honor and best bud safely held the actual rings, giving the ring bearer two decoys in a little blue box. Five-year-olds look adorable in suits or dresses but shouldn't be entrusted with diamonds and gold bands.

The priest asked the ringbearer to come forward for his big moment. He squeezed between two of the best buds and came to stand slightly to the right of the couple, smiling enthusiastically at the two brides. Usually, a ring bearer anxiously hands off his pillow or box to a member of the wedding party before sheepishly scooting back to his parents or grandparents. But this little boy didn't want to miss out on a thing and decided to stay and watch.

The officiant walked each bride through the designated words as she presented a pretend ring to her betrothed, while the ring bearer looked up at them in wonder. He knew something special was happening here, that he had an important job and played a part in a significant moment. I watched him instead of the brides, his eyes wide and full of curiosity and inquisitiveness. He wasn't marveling that two brides comprised the wedding couple. Instead, he wore the same look of most other ring bearers, trying to figure out what made this moment so meaningful. He watched, learning about love and the weight of two people's commitment when they deeply love each other.

Hopefulness washed over me. Plenty of news today intends to discourage, and even though I don't watch or listen to most of it, it still makes me anxious and even frightened at times. I begin to despair of people and lose hope in humanity, feeling that we seem hell-bent on ruining all of creation and hurting one another. But then I remember this little boy standing there, eyes full of wonder, and my heart softens. In that moment, hope returned to me, and the memory continues to renew my faith in this world, especially in the younger generations.

That little boy will never know a time when the law prevented people of the same gender from proclaiming their love for one another in a marriage ceremony, recognized by the state as a sign of their commitment, on equal footing as every couple of opposite gender. For him, two women are as much a married couple as a man and a woman, same as for two men. He will only know the improved reality of this positive change, as do my own children. My kids have grown up with friends with two mommies or two daddies and friends with a mommy and a daddy, and now, as teenagers, they have friends across the gender and sexuality spectrums.

A change in the law, though, does not precipitate immediate changes in the heart. The father of one of the brides initially threatened to boycott the wedding. He worked most of his life as a Southern Baptist preacher, condemning homosexuality throughout his ministry. Many preachers found "gay marriage" as an abstract concept easier to argue against than when it became a reality in their own homes. Seeing it in action defied and began to challenge long-held theological beliefs.

Understandably, we hold our beliefs and doctrines tightly; they become a part of our identity, and any threat to them threatens our sense of being. Many family members of LGBTQ+ people have struggled with the conflict between inherited limiting beliefs and the reality of witnessing love in action. I cannot minimize this struggle with any fairness. When we grow up hearing one thing and then watch it actively and effectively dismantled, the tension between feeling loyal to the old ways and the truth in the new requires thoughtful and often demanding reflection.

In the case of the Tennessee wedding, the father set aside his objections, agreeing to come but not to participate. Likely, he realized it would be hard to live with the regret of not attending his daughter's wedding and endure her and his wife's disappointment. I watched him during the rehearsal as he absorbed and learned along with the little ring bearer. His expression differed markedly from the little boy's, but he thoughtfully observed the activity all the same.

Later, during the ceremony, I continued to glance at him, noting the change in his demeanor. Witnessing the depth of love shared between his daughter and her bride softened him. He could not escape the warm wave of genuine affection that settled on us, prompting many of us to shed tears of joy.

Unfortunately, other commitments required me to leave soon after giving an invocation at the reception. I stood by the door to the barn, not ready to go. As music filled the room, I looked as this same father, the one who, until the last minute, refused to come, caught his daughter up for a traditional father-daughter dance for all to see. Midway through their dance, I turned and left for home but, later, I learned that after he danced with his daughter, he asked to dance with her bride as well. Thinking about it now still brings tears to my eyes. By the grace of God, people change, we change, and the world changes.

The mother hen of grace and love determinedly pulls us all under her wing, regardless of our efforts to resist. God wants us together, celebrating love at every turn. We need these moments, these brides, the little ring bearer, and the reconciled father. We need to see the power of the Spirit working in the world in our best interest, marching us towards justice and love, regardless of our rebellions.

I'm Sorry, I Can't.

Forming and encouraging disciples for the work of ministry in the world comprises a significant part of a pastor's job. We dedicate seasons and Sundays in our preaching and teaching to guide church members in discerning a call to engage in new ministries. Annual fall stewardship campaigns focus on the members' financial responsibility to the church, but we also address how they offer their time and talent to the community. By sharing our spiritual gifts and taking time out of our busy schedules, we can accomplish the work of God in the world.

Despite this work's worthy and essential nature, most people must be encouraged and asked to become more involved in the church's life. Churchgoers take time to settle. Some people attend for years before joining any ministry, considering themselves outsiders long after pastors and church staff count them as members. The step from "attendee" to "active member" feels too large for many. Newcomers also struggle to identify which of their identities could benefit the shared life of the church. As a pastor, I regularly thought of the congregation and individuals' spiritual gifts, then personally asked them to share their talents for a specific class, activity, or project. A frequent refrain among church leaders trying to encourage greater participation is, "People like to be asked."

However, pastors have a less frequent but no less important

conversation, often in the privacy of the pastor's office. Generally, it starts when a relatively new member calls and makes an appointment with the pastor to discuss the church. The reason given might be to learn more about the church family and its many ministries. The person arrives and pleasantly talks about her history of attending church, where she came from, how she's been involved in past churches, and how much she loves her new church.

Then, often sheepishly, comes the request for forgiveness. The new member shares that she has been through a difficult time. She details her hardships, then quickly adds, " I'm not telling you all this to get your sympathy or for you to pray for me; I'll be fine. I just wanted you to know because, right now, I just can't be as involved as I usually am. I'm so sorry." Recalling these confessions and the apparent embarrassment and guilt with which the people offered them pains me still.

First, let us celebrate the commitment at the heart of this apology. Anyone who comes to the pastor to ask forgiveness for not being as involved as she thinks she should fully understands and embraces her call to discipleship. She represents the goal for the rest of us. At some point, she heard and internalized the message that the church represents the body of Christ in the world and that God's work only occurs if we are the ones to do it. You go, girl! Pass the word to others!

Next, the church needs to reexamine its lack of balance between labor and rest. Habitually, Christian leadership preaches on the importance of hands-on, lived ministry without granting equal emphasis on the importance of the Sabbath. We let our frustration with those who express no desire to share in the work impede our obligation to care for those who do too much. I freely admit I share the blame here. If someone comes forward again and again with passion and volunteers to be a part of almost every ministry, I get excited. The energy and excitement of visionaries and doers drive the work forward. They're the ones I want on a committee or in charge of a project, because they'll get it done and do it with joy, inviting others to become involved. But, sometimes, I need to set boundaries for such a person instead of urging her ever forward, because she may not be setting them for herself.

Once the new member apologizes, I see her face covered in guilt and sadness. She braces herself for a word from me about responsibility and involvement, some chastisement for her lacking sense of duty. Maybe she worries that in the best scenario, I will respond, "Well, okay, I guess. We can give you a month or two of rest, but you must get back at it as soon as possible." Instead, I assure her that her feelings are valid and that it's okay to take a step back when needed. I thank her for her honesty and willingness to share, and I remind her that God calls us to various ministries in the seasons of our lives. In some seasons, we can be on the ball, as it were. We have the energy and strength to serve on four committees and give two days a week to volunteer around the church grounds. During these active seasons, we happily offer much to the collective work of the church body.

But other periods demand rest. We use a holy and blessed word for this—"Sabbath." It refers not only to the one day of the week we (supposedly) set aside for rest but also to entire seasons. These periods of Sabbath often follow turbulent and busy times. Perhaps someone suffered a serious illness or walked the path of hospice care and death with a loved one. Another person may have downsized after forty years of living in a larger home, and that change brought relief and loss. Still, another might be marking one year of sobriety by taking life one day at a time and needing less, rather than more, to deal with. These are exhausting processes.

I tell this to the new member in my office and share it with you: If you find yourself "empty" and unable to be active in church, it's okay. Sometimes, God calls us to sit on several committees, sing in the choir, help with the capital campaign, and stand for election to the church governance committee. But other times, God calls us into a season of quiet; in those times, our job is to show up and sit in the pews.

Our culture overvalues action and undervalues the Sabbath. We applaud people for giving time and a half or more than 100% while judging the perceived "pewsitter" as lazy and selfish. We desperately need examples from our brothers, sisters, and siblings who model self-care and Sabbath-keeping. We believe in resurrection and restoration but don't know how to do it. For this reason, We need people like this newcomer in the pews among us, engaging fully in the contemplation of worship while allowing herself a season of re-creation and nourishment.

If you find yourself in a sabbath season, please do not apologize. You have a ministry, one that models embracing the call to quietude and mending.

Bumper Cars and Spider Webs

I stand, arms crossed on the metal railing, as I watch the red car with lightning bolts head straight for the yellow vehicle painted with the words "crash!" and "pow!" Fellow amusement park enthusiasts have climbed in and now look devilishly at one another, pushing their little cars as fast as they will go, straight for one another. The drivers burst into laughter as the thick rubber bumpers around their cars make contact and jolt the vehicles apart. Only space exists between the cars where, for a split second, they become one mass of metal and rubber. Still laughing, the drivers turn their attention to other vehicles and drivers. A socially acceptable maniacal obsession overtakes them as they plunge themselves once again into the fray.

We place a high premium on rugged individualism in the United States. We prize gumption and exalt people who seem to conquer life all by themselves. We crave stories of survivors who have escaped the worst situations with little more than their bare hands. I chalk it up to collective pride in our history of carving a great nation out of a wild and untamed land. I, too, want to know that I could take care of myself if placed in a genuinely arduous situation. It's the reason I like to learn new skills.

Unfortunately, our hyper-focus on the individual often leads us past the desired sense of self-sufficiency and into the realm of alienation and isolation. In our minds, we become too accustomed to thinking of ourselves as autonomous. We draw thick lines around ourselves, imagining these lines shield us. We pretend they serve as bumpers, allowing us to safely bounce off others unscathed. The wrong ideals and impurities of those we encounter slide off our perceived protective lines.

Despite what our shared cultural delusion would have us believe, we do not simply bounce off one another to find emptiness return between us as before we met. There are no lines. There are no bumpers. We reinforce this delusion by lauding people we describe as having "thick skin." We marvel at individuals who seem to bounce off the worst of life with nary a scratch, not a tear shed or a scar to show for it. These types successfully draw impenetrable lines around themselves, and we admire their strength.

But we are not bumper cars. We are spiders. We leave a trail of webbing behind us that never breaks. It may fade but never severs. Our lives touch another's, and we lay down a pinpoint, a marker that we have been there, and our silken web moves forward from that place. We do not bounce off one another. We touch and part, not to find empty space, but two threads, one from us and one from the other. Forever, our lives connect, no matter how tenuously. We may bear scars from the contact or be strengthened by it. Even if we never remember it, our encounter changes us, even if in infinitesimal ways.

People who rode on a plane with you, the clerk in the gas station, your third-grade teacher, the girl in college you eyed in your history class but never spoke to, the child in the store who looked at you for comfort when he had lost his mother--you now share a thread connecting you to each one of them. We may try to break these threads or pretend they do not exist, but the Spirit created them, and our power is nothing compared to hers. The threads may weaken, but they never disappear entirely, try as we might to erase them.

In the eleventh chapter of the book of Numbers Moses laments about the complaints of his people. He tires of hearing them speak of their enslavement in Egypt as if it were infinitely better than their wandering in the desert. Moses asks God, "Why have you mistreated your servant? Why have I not found favor in your sight that you lay the burden of all these people on me? Did I conceive all these people? Did I give birth to them, that you should say to me, 'Carry them in your bosom, as a nurse carries a sucking child,' to the land that you promised on oath to their ancestors?"

Dear, faithful Moses. We have heard your argument before. We listen to it daily: "I'm not their parent; why should I have to take care of them? I don't have any kids; why should I pay for their education? Where are that child's parents to teach them better? Parents today are failing their children. If I were their parent, you better believe they wouldn't act like that. At the very least, our teachers should be doing a better job so kids today aren't running wild, so disrespectful."

Moses, you did not carry the Israelites in your womb. You will never know the honor and pain of carrying and bearing a child. That blessing belongs to Zipporah. But you are their father, nonetheless, because you draw breath. God made you responsible for them because you are a spider, Moses, and your life will be connected to theirs forever, as theirs will be to yours. The Spirit blessed you with life and charged you to care for all of creation, the same as she created and charges every person who has life.

My friends, the bumpers are myths. Indeed, as you read these words, you and I are connected. No space exists between us, just as no space exists between you and anyone else who might read this. The silken webs of billions of beautifully unique spiders cover our world. We may not see them, but they call out to us in varied and unexpected ways. "Do not forget me," cries the memory of a grandparent. "Care for me," cries the line to the stranger who feels lonely and hurt. We hear, "Be blessed and loved," in the vibrations sent over the connection from a most beloved friend.

May we strive not to forget who we are. May we tend our threads and accept the love and care from those at the other end. May we grow more intentional about how and why we place our pinpoints, our newest connections, for through them, we change one another's lives.

Savor

I have the blessing of raising three amazing kids. They make me laugh, hold me accountable, and keep me busy. Depending on how I count them, I also work three jobs. Some days keep me close to home as I arrange pork and beef sales for our farm or do research for the farm store, which we hope to open one day soon. Other days take me two or more hours from home to lead workshops, speak at events, or supply for other clergy as they take much-needed vacations. Business lunches, podcast recording, the too-rare hour or two to write, and occasional home repairs eat up the rest of my time.

Mornings in my house can be catch-as-catch-can. The kids know where to find breakfast cereal, milk, or protein bars. Depending on the day, various combinations of inhabitants might leave the house at two or three different times. Many look a little like this:

"Where's your backpack? I need backpacks, y'all!"

"Pack a snack for yourself."

"Mama, some people eat two snacks at snack time. . ."

"No, you may not pack two snacks. One is fine."

"Have you brushed your hair?"

"Yes!"

"Are you sure?"

"We're too late to sit for cereal breakfast; grab a protein bar on the way out the door."

"Ugh! I don't like that kind!"

"Next time, get up and get dressed early enough for a bowl of cereal!"

Then, just as I think we're too hurried, too harried, and chaos has taken the reigns, one of my kids walks up to me, getting my attention.

"What do you need?" I say, exasperated.

"Nothing."

"Why are you standing here?"

"I just want to give you a hug."

I wrap my arms around her. The tight string that had pulled my entire body towards the ceiling with anxiety and stress suddenly releases. My blood pressure drops as I curve my body around the shape of her and rest my cheek on her shoulder.

Savor. "Savor this," I tell myself.

We cannot savor in a hurry. This action demands time and passivity, requiring attention and intentionality. It's not so much an action word as one about receiving. Savor.

I often struggle to remember the last time I savored a meal. Most days, I barely register the flavor of the food as it passes over my tongue. For too many meals, I eat while I also carry on conversations, make sure my kids eat, or respond to emails and texts. Like most of life's actions, eating becomes a perfunctory process.

We savor to get the whole flavor of a thing:

- A glass of wine.

- A bite of perfect soft cheese.

- The first tomato sandwich of the summer (white bread, tomato, plenty of black pepper, and always, ever, only Duke's mayo).

We take a bite and chew, but our taste buds do the passive work of registering the complex flavors. The molecules of sour, sweet, buttery, and peppery all pass over those tiny buds on our tongues, which then send signals of delight or distaste to our brains. We reflexively chew and let the receptors do the rest.

When my child comes in for a hug, my job is to passively receive it. Once I complete the active work of wrapping my body around them, my involuntary response systems take over. The moment arrives to savor and breathe. The signals up my neural pathways push my brain to shed some stress and give up its marathon mode. My body responds, releasing more of itself into the embrace.

"Savor" sounds like a pretentious word reserved for meals of luxury or wines aged to peak perfection. We consider it a luxury we should only indulge in once we have earned it through our productivity. In other words, subconsciously, we believe we have neither the time nor the right to do it. "Savor" is for the frivolous enjoyment of luxuries, not for practical people.

No, friends, we wrongly treat it as an occasional indulgence. Savoring is a necessity. "Savor" is only one letter away from "Savior." We must be stopped, saved from ourselves and our desire to go-go-go and learn, instead, to be more passive, to revel in sensations and responses outside our control or doing.

I imagine Jesus reclined at the Passover table with his friends. They ate delicious food prepared out of thanksgiving and remembrance. Because he knew this was his last meal with his friends, he savored that night. We hear this in the different gospel accounts showing how he lovingly showered affection, wisdom, and encouragement on his disciples. He valued each moment.

Then, I think of the disciples and how they saw it as a Passover meal like the ones they shared before and would after. They ate the expected foods, with Jesus throwing in an odd word or action. I imagine the crumbs falling from their mouths in their eagerness to argue with one another and interrupt Jesus to disagree. Did they register the taste of a single bite that night? Did they later regret not savoring those last hours they had with Christ?

Savoring is no luxury but a necessity. We need to resist getting so caught up in our doing that we miss receiving the gift of the moment. Our souls and spirits need more passivity, the action or inaction to receive whatever the world has to offer, letting the little gifts of touch, interaction, and joy wash over us. We must learn the discipline of giving our mind a quiet space to process and fire off synapses that turn moments into memories.

Savor, savor every day, my friends.

The Unbearable, Relatable All-Or-Nothing of Peter

Modern Americans live by an understood creed that, if you dare to do something, you better get it right the first time. Great coaches and leadership experts constantly preach the importance of failing because our society constantly reinforces the opposite for us. "Go big or go home," "This ain't my first rodeo," "fish or cut bait," and "always give it 100%" send the clear message that we must act fast, act decisively, act with expertise (even if we have zero), and act with complete commitment. The all-or-nothing world only allows for success or crippling failure. Either you triumph or you fall. This attitude leaves no room for the reality of the in-between, those steps that led from A to Z where we do our best learning and growing. The Apostle Peter would have made a great American in the 21st century.

Peter, the disciple-turned-apostle-turned-rock of the church, lives and dies by this mentality. He witnesses the transfiguration, and rather than speaking with Jesus, listening and learning, he babbles, "Let's make this permanent! Freeze this moment in time and turn this place into a shrine!"

In another story, Peter looks out from the boat to see Jesus walking on water and says, "I gotta do that!" Which he does—until he doesn't. All in, he steps out of the boat onto the waves and strides towards Jesus. Then, remembering the impossibility of such a feat, he panics and loses every morsel of confidence. He finds himself sinking fast, headed for a drowning. Blessedly, Jesus reaches forth a hand and lifts him up again.

At what becomes known as the Last Supper, Jesus informs the disciples he wants to wash their feet. Peter, in nothing mode, protests because, well, that's nasty and below Jesus. When Jesus responds that his disciples must be washed in order to be part of him, all-in Peter jumps forward, demanding that his teacher wash not only his feet but his entire body.

Jesus warns Peter that he will deny his rabbi three times before the rooster crows during the night spanning Maundy Thursday to Good Friday. Aspirationally perfect, Peter denies the possibility of the denials, proclaiming a total commitment to Jesus. Within short order, Peter begins his triple rejection. Consistently, Peter shows he knows neither how to comply nor disobey partially. When he does something, he does it with authority and enthusiasm.

I often imagine Jesus shaking his head at Peter, fighting back the urge to say, "Ugh! Peter, can you just not? Could you dial it back just this once?" In a marvelous passage that both startles and amuses, Peter reprimands Jesus for prophesying his death, and Jesus, having run out of patience, turns to him with the strongest rebuke imaginable, "Get behind me, Satan!"

According to legend, Peter even died all in. Whereas other apostles suffered beheadings, stonings, and crucifixion, Peter found himself not only on a cross but one posted upside down.

Generally, I appreciate the intention behind the all-or-nothing mentality. Our best hope at succeeding lies in giving it our best effort and whole heart. Watch any amateur sporting event and notice how the athletes who struggle most, generally show the least confidence. Their confidence affects their performance, not the other way around. Timidity reduces the likelihood that a player will hit the ball, make the basket, block the shot, or ace the serve.

But what works best on the court, pitch, or field does not necessarily work best in life. All-or-nothing closes us off to growth and learning. Our brains focus on possible success or failure, paying most attention to getting it "right," and we can't step back for objectivity to teach us. We think, "I've got to get this right," or "People will ridicule me if I fail," leaving no room for observation, processing, or humor. The fear of failure shuts us down, and we would go home empty-handed, empty-hearted, and empty-headed rather than open our eyes, ears, and minds to learn whatever lessons the experience of defeat scatters about in front of us.

A prayer in the Anglican and Episcopal traditions about the importance of scriptures asks God to help us "hear them, read, mark, learn, and inwardly digest them." That process becomes increasingly difficult if we begin from the assumption that we have the "right" and "wrong" ways of interpreting them. If I enter a situation presuming what both failure and success look like, I cannot be open to recognizing, much less absorbing, the many lessons cast in my path.

"All or nothing" sounds confident and committed and makes for a great slogan but a terrible approach to much of life. Peter ends up the buffoon in a number of the gospel stories because of his dogged commitment to this mentality. He becomes the foil from which generations of Christians learn how not to respond to Jesus. If only we actually learned that lesson.

The good news is that Peter still becomes the "rock" of the church, that his misguided ego cannot stop the power of the Holy Spirit. God moves and works through us despite our limited human perspective. But God also encourages us to embrace the philosophy of enough over the philosophy of everything. One step, one seed, one word of love becomes all God needs to germinate the Kingdom of God. Maybe one day, we'll learn to stop insisting on the marathon, the industrial farm, and the one-thousand-word soliloquy and settle for the stroll, the container garden on the deck, and a child's giggle.

A Good Word Not for Me

I confess that the Jesus in Mark's gospel is not my favorite. We have four versions of Christ, one per gospel, and they run the spectrum from Mark to John. John's Jesus feels ethereal at times and a bit fluffy. I love John's gospel, but I find his Jesus unrelatable, a bit too heavy on divinity and light on humanity. Luke and Matthew sit in the middle, portraying Jesus with a nice balance as someone who can become passionate at times but also who performs incredible miracles while preaching good, mostly understandable, sermons. Arguably, they domesticate Jesus too much, but that makes them more comfortable to me.

Mark's Jesus, on the other hand, feels gritty and raw. He's in a hurry, rushing from place to place, and comes across as short-tempered and testy. The Christ of Mark says things I don't like. He appears rude and uncouth, as in Mark 3:20-35:

"and the crowd came together again, so that they could not even eat. When his family heard it, they went out to restrain him, for people were saying, 'He has gone out of his mind.' And the scribes who came down from Jerusalem said, 'He has Beelzebul, and by the ruler of the demons he casts out demons.' And he called them to him, and spoke to them in parables, 'How can Satan cast out Satan? If a kingdom is divided against itself, that kingdom cannot stand. And if a house is divided against itself, that house will not be *able to stand. And if Satan has risen up against himself and is divided, he cannot stand, but his end has come. But no one can enter a strong man's house and plunder his property without first tying up the strong man; then indeed the house can be plundered.*

'Truly I tell you, people will be forgiven for their sins and whatever blasphemies they utter; but whoever blasphemes against the Holy Spirit can never have forgiveness, but is guilty of an eternal sin'— for they had said, 'He has an unclean spirit.'

Then his mother and his brothers came; and standing outside, they sent to him and called him. A crowd was sitting around him; and they said to him, 'Your mother and your brothers and sisters[a] are outside, asking for you.' And he replied, 'Who are my mother and my brothers?' And looking at those who sat around him, he said, 'Here are my mother and my brothers! Whoever does the will of God is my brother and sister and mother.'

The first paragraph above makes sense to me. People around Jesus have started talking about his behavior, claiming he must be possessed to do and say what he does. They claim either Satan or a demon has mastery over him, controlling his behavior. Jesus offers a sound rebuttal: how can Satan cast himself out? If Satan turns against himself, then the whole thing collapses. A house divided cannot stand; therefore, their logic doesn't hold up because demonic forces wouldn't drive out other sinister forces.

His mother and brothers come to speak with him and perhaps implore him to stop. Remember, Mark's gospel begins with Jesus's baptism. Because it does not have a birth narrative, we know little about the Mary of Mark. I imagine her appearance here stems from a desire to grab Jesus by the ear and pull him out of the crowd for misbehaving. In my mind, a nicer version has her sitting down with him to express her concern and learn why he feels compelled to do such work.

Whatever the case, Jesus rejects his family at the end of the selection mentioned above. People in the crowd notify him that his mom and siblings have arrived, to which he says, "Who are my mother and my brothers?" Looking at those who sat around him, he adds, "Here are my mother and my brothers! Whoever does the will of God is my brother and sister and mother."

I grew up in Georgia, and where I'm from, that will not do. Not only does he refuse an audience with them, he doesn't even acknowledge the validity of their relationship! One thing you do not do is talk bad about your family, especially in public. You aren't supposed to do it even in private. You don't talk bad about your mama, and absolutely do not fail to acknowledge her existence in front of a room full of people! This Jesus goes too far in acting rudely towards his family and offends my sensibilities.

Then I remember that not every word in the Bible was written for me. Shocking, I know, but not all of it applies to my life; the Spirit inspired words to speak to others and their experiences and needs.

Over the twenty years of my priesthood, some of the most rewarding and heartbreaking work I've been blessed with has been welcoming Spiritual Refugees into the church: people who have had the experience of either feeling uncomfortable or unwelcome in a past church. Even worse, some have been told they aren't "allowed" to be a part of that church anymore, including, in some cases, the churches of their childhood. They have experienced rejection for a variety of reasons and are left traumatized by this spiritual abuse.

For example, many people who identify as LGBTQIA+ find themselves without a spiritual home after they come out to friends and family. They spend their most formative years learning about the unconditional love of God only to have their church family show them limited love and a willingness to exclude them for merely being as God created them. Some of these siblings didn't experience a cold shoulder or being uninvited to events. For some, church pastors and elders told them to leave and never come back unless they "repented" and turned from their ways, which would mean denying their very identity.

And this is just one example. My denomination, the Episcopal Church, has received riches in the form of women of other denominations seeking to become priests, thanks to their churches that deny the ordination of women. Many of my sisters of the cloth still love the denomination and theology of their childhood, but came to us because their church rejected them for being honest about their calling to preach the Good News and lead worship. I raise prayers of thanksgiving for those churches' failure to recognize my friends' callings, because we have received some incredible leaders and preachers as a result.

Twenty years ago, soon after my ordination, I met more people than I do today who had to leave their church homes because of divorce or for marrying the wrong person. Some churches forbade divorce under any circumstances and excommunicated divorcees. Others refused to recognize marriages to people "outside the faith," meaning marrying someone of another religion, or for some Protestants marrying a Catholic.

One of my more heartbreaking encounters came early in my ministry when I heard a knock at the door of my office. I opened it to find one of my older parishioners in tears and welcomed her in. She continued to cry during our two-hour conversation. That day marked the tenth anniversary of her husband's death by suicide due to depression. The church she had left told her that he would burn in hell forever for dying by his own hand and that she needed to accept she would never see him again. Ten years later, that "truth" weighed her in inconceivable ways. She came to me as a last effort to hear that another theological perspective existed, one that provided forgiveness for him and the chance for them to see each other in the afterlife.

I have had the pleasure of welcoming many people into the Episcopal Church who have made their last attempt at finding a spiritual home with us. New members have told me they had heard the Episcopal Church was different, often said with a scandalous rather than winsome tone, and thought they would give church one last chance. They said, if they hadn't found a place with us, they never would have stepped foot in another church again.

What Jesus says about his brothers, sisters, and mother sounds very different to someone who has lived one of these experiences. Imagine how it would feel to be told by your family, birth or spiritual, that they no longer welcome you, that you do not belong with them. For someone cast out by their family of origin, hearing Jesus say, "Don't worry about them! You are MY people now. You belong with ME now. You ARE my family, and you belong with me," comes as a balm. Jesus turns from asking, "Who are my mother and my brothers?" about his birth family to face his new community, proclaiming, "Here are my mother and my brothers! Whoever does the will of God is my brother and sister and mother." His action rings true and resonates with those rejected by family and cast out by the very people who swore to love them. Jesus says to each one of us, "You belong with me forever and longer. You are my brother, my sister, my sibling. You are the adopted child of God. You are BELOVED, and you belong."

I find it miraculous that our holy scripture shares God's truth with everyone differently. This library of books collected over thousands of years and passed down to us over thousands of years continues to speak to us, each in personal and genuine ways, by the power of the Holy Spirit. What might be uncomfortable for me becomes the most healing word another child of God might hear their entire life.

Not every word was written specifically for me or for you, but for all of us. The Bible provides a collection of stories that can bring the most needed word in our hour of discomfort and the most unsettling word in our hour of complacency. Marvelous.

Loving the Story, Inspiring Play

We spend several Saturdays every summer retrieving my oldest from church camp. I realize "church camp" conjures various images for people, and, likely, this particular church camp doesn't match any of them. For us, church camp looks a lot like the traditional summer camps of yesteryear but with a splash of God thrown in for good measure. Most weeks, campers begin their day with rowdy morning singing led by a staff that hypes them up for the rest of the day. Next comes the "dean's program," when volunteer leaders come from churches around the diocese with a team of others to engage the kids in spiritual learning while having fun. In the afternoons, the campers enjoy all the traditional camp trappings, such as outdoor games, pool time, arts and crafts, and visits to the neighboring nature center to pet snakes and learn about the local ecosystem. The staffers and counselors put on fun evening activities like carnivals, movie and skit nights, or s'mores around the campfire before nighttime singing and lights out.

Over my years in ministry, I worked as a seminarian and then as dean at three different Episcopal camps, all of which shared a similar structure. Campers come to enjoy some of the last vestiges of unadulterated and non-agenda-fied summer fun. No one attends these camps to add impressive accomplishments to their transcripts for college applications, try out the latest tech advances, or network with other future corporate bigwigs. They don't work on their golf or tennis games or improve their test scores to improve college acceptance rates. Serving at these camps gave me some of the most fun and free weeks of my ministry.

One of my oldest child's favorite camp sessions includes a dean's program focused entirely on the performing arts. Before jumping to conclusions, let me specify that no campers attended this session as a springboard for Broadway stardom. They don't even participate as a springboard to their elementary or middle school drama programs. The dean's staff organizes this week purely for the joy of singing, dancing, acting, and puppeteering. Psalm 100 specifies, "Make a joyful NOISE unto the Lord"; therefore, we should sing, act, and dance with abandon, harboring no fear in our hearts for what others might think.

Every year, Performing Arts Camp (PA Camp, as it is affectionately known) takes a familiar story from the Bible and assigns segments to groups of campers for them to portray on stage. The staffers and counselors help write the script and guide the campers, producing an end performance that comes off like a string of skits, loosely assembled, which is precisely what it is. Over the week, the campers practice their parts, create set pieces, find props, and choreograph dances. Friends and family come on Saturday morning to watch the finished product.

One year's performance hilariously portrayed the Easter story from before the events of Palm Sunday to the Ascension. That's right, I said, "hilarious." I laughed at the cleverness of the writing and the adept ways the campers pulled off magnificent comedic timing. Judas, especially, had me in stitches as the little girl who portrayed him threw herself into her part. I never imagined I could enjoy Judas so much. I laughed entirely too loudly at a particularly well-timed line delivered by a sock puppet when one asked another to read the lips of two other conspiring characters, and the other replied, "Don't ask me. We're sock puppets. Every word looks the same."

As the show moved forward, I wondered how they would manage the crucifixion. The performance thus far had me smiling and engaged in the story, but I worried about how deftly they would shift to heavier subject matter. The singing group transitioned us with a version of Boulevard of Broken Dreams by Greenday, in which they rewrote the lyrics to suit Jesus on his way to the cross. The line "I walk a lonely road" took on a whole new meaning and transitioned our mindset without making us feel guilty for having enjoyed ourselves up to this point. Then, the dancers took the stage to portray the crucifixion of Christ in a way that held loosely the heartbreak of the historic event while honoring the beautiful, inevitable lightness of a small group of sweaty campers dancing on stage at the end of a fun week together.

After the performance, the serving interim director of the camp and conference center and I talked about the campers and how well they did. She and I share a history of working in the diocese together, and I enjoyed catching up with her. We laughed about the skillful way the campers, staff, and counselors handled the material, including some of its irreverence. She smiled and said, "But they got the story."

And that's just it. They got the story, and in a way they never will forget because they were allowed to play in it, move around in it, and claim it as their own. I did not experience that privilege until I became a seminarian, and my professors reintroduced me to the joy of the scriptures. Between my studious nature and how my Sunday school teachers presented the Bible, I thought such fun must be blasphemous. Studying scripture should only be done thoughtfully, reverently, without question or examination, and under the tutelage of a wise expert; no laughing allowed.

Don't get me wrong, I had marvelous Sunday school teachers. To this day, I run into them at events in my hometown and love getting hugs from them. They would pinch my cheeks, I think, if they could reach them. They loved me and sharing the Good News with my classes. However, the structure of the curriculum and its desire to instill in us a profound and hefty respect for the importance of the text often tied their hands, limiting their ability to show us how we could play in the story. I certainly couldn't see myself in the events that happened to those people too many years ago for any of them to be relevant to me and my life. I didn't feel important enough to be counted among the characters in this saga that spanned generations and generations.

But the importance of the collection of stories we call the "Bible" does not necessitate binding it in chains and covering it in velvet, allowing ourselves mere glances on days when our souls are "right," which is not often. Because of their importance, they should dance in our imaginations, not just exist as still frames in our collective memory. The psalmists should sing out with us in our shouts of giggles and our cries of lament. The nativity should have rowdy sheep played by toddlers who cry and wet their costumes and angels who think their names are "Herald" because that's what the song says. I want my feet to feel wet with Peter's when he walks on water, my fear to well up when I remember that we can't, and relief to wash over me when Jesus pulls us from the water. Dripping wet and relieved, we remember that Jesus has us, even when we lose ourselves.

The Bible better serves us as a sandbox of faith rather than a monolith of unquestionable wisdom. Let the stories sift through your fingers, watch the smaller bits fall through, and pay attention to the treasures left in the palm of your hand. Build castles out of the legends of Ester and David, then laugh at the comedic anti-hero of Jonah. Tear down the walls of Jericho by crashing like wild things through the piles of sand you built with buckets, and then carve a river with water from the hose to float baby Moses down the Nile once more.

Play in the story so it may be yours, and you understand how we add to it, even if only in infinitesimal ways, by our own living and breathing . . . and playing.

Not Your Time. Not Your Place. Not Your Call.

I quickly become engrossed in other people's projects. Tell me about your latest hobby or passion, and I'll sit for over an hour, asking you questions and trying my best to act like I possess some knowledge on the subject. Perhaps you found your mother's old embroidery kit and decided to pick it up. Describe to me the intricacies of it, how you came to discover this latest pleasure, what you're learning about it, and the fruit you're bearing from your efforts, and I will listen with rapt attention. By the time I go home, I likely will have decided that your hobby du jour should become mine. As I pull in my car to park beside my house, I will have planned how I will teach myself embroidery, which decorative items and articles of clothing I will adorn, what homemade gifts I will create and wrap for friends and family this Christmas, and will have placed in my cart a starter embroidery kit on Amazon.

I blame my ADHD. I love to start activities, get bored by the middle, and must push myself to finish almost every project I begin. Halfway through many of my latest and greatest nonessential passions, my brain flips its working center to autopilot so the creative side can start asking, "What next?" Sometimes, I focus on the working part and leave the creative side to play in its sandbox of imaginings. Still, other times, the productive brain becomes neglected, and I take for granted its ability to function without me.

I even stopped writing at this point in this reflection to play with my son. He's excited about his new video game, enough to endure allowing me to join on occasion. He asked me earlier in the day to hop in on a level of one of his favorites, and I got as far as the third paragraph here before deciding I needed to be there with him. My passion for writing never ends, but that doesn't make it immune to my lack of focus some days. I find the siren song of something new and novel too challenging to resist.

There's also the comparison problem that ensnares my attention. I see someone in a similar role doing something I am not, and I fall into the temptation of thinking I should also be doing it. If she is a mother and doing this "motherly" activity, am I failing in my role as a mother if I am not doing the same? What about as a priest? If they are traveling to this or that pilgrimage site, publishing this or that sort of book, or championing this or that cause, I need to do the same instead. Mom, writer, friend, priest, farmer, concerned citizen—all of these roles open a myriad of opportunities for me to find new distractions or reasons to doubt my efficacy in doing my part for my family, friends, or the greater good.

We bump into David's distractibility in the Hebrew Scripture reading for this Sunday. By the time we encounter King David, he's done some things. He has experienced military success, uniting the tribes of Israel into one nation. He's captured Jerusalem and established it as the royal city, bringing the ark of the Lord to rest within its walls. At this point, David can feel satisfied by his work as the King of God's people. We meet up with him as he realizes he has a house made of cedar, but God's ark remains in a tent. David seeks the council of the prophet Nathan on how best to build a more appropriate home for God.

God answers clearly, "I haven't asked you to do that. I have freely been among you, supporting and encouraging you, and now you want to put me in a home? Not yet. That's not your work. Listen, your line will be successful, and someone else can think about building a temple. Now is not your time, not your place, not your call."

We hear a similar sentiment at the end of the book of Deuteronomy as God stands with Moses after all his wandering in the desert, looking out on the promised land. God shows Moses the land and says, "'This is the land which I swore to Abraham, Isaac, and Jacob, saying 'I will give it to your descendants.' I have let you see it with your eyes, but you shall not go over there." (Deuteronomy 34:4). Moses had the task of liberating the people and seeing them safely through the wilderness. He can be proud of his vocation and time as a great prophet, but leadership past that point belongs to someone else. It is not his time, not his place, not his call.

Our willingness to recognize when a project is not ours to tackle can be as challenging as identifying one in the first place. While working with boards, organizations, and churches, I get most excited by groups that see beyond limits and allow opportunities to unfold in front of them. These bands of visionaries make for the most fun during any brainstorming session. With only one or two questions to spark their imaginations, they take off with one another with exclamations of, "We could do that!" and "Oh! What about this?" Within ten short minutes, they identify needs in the community they could address, activities they could share, and events they could host. I much prefer time spent madly exploring the sky's limits and beyond with can-do groups as opposed to ones who reluctantly speak about what "we" might do, when all the while they mean one or two specific people while they sit back and watch. Or, worse, ones that stare across the table at one another saying, "I don't know. What do you want to do?" or "I don't know. We've never done that before."

The challenge for the most energetic and enthusiastic boards and organizations is understanding that not all work is meant for everyone. We might map out fifteen possible paths to take and have fun imagining each potential journey's shape. I find it painful sometimes to point out to visionary groups that, though they find energy in entertaining 100 ideas, other people within their community might already be undertaking the work they imagine and might be doing it better. Though these bands of go-getters have it within their capacity to tackle a specific project or community issue, that does not make it suitable for them. The opportunity to launch a new thing becomes an invitation to support and partner in a project in progress and concede that someone else needs to be in charge.

I resonate so well with this challenge for brainstorming enthusiasts and those imagining what else might be. Of all the social media outlets I use, I am the worst at remembering to post on LinkedIn, despite their persistence in vying for my attention. They send me updates stating how many "searches" accessed my profile and lists of job openings their algorithms deem right for me. I can't help but open them. I don't care much about the searches, but the job listings trigger my creative brain to map out an entirely different vocation and life for myself and my family. I get inside the description, learn about the company, and my mind has us packed up and moving to Alaska to work for some publishing house or church or remaining put with me sitting at home, quietly doing data entry or training AI in conversational English from the comfort of my farm.

But then I hear the Spirit whisper, "Not your time. Not your place. Not your call." I just know I could do 100 jobs better than those who actually work them. And that crusade for a good cause? Surely, they need my help! I'm also sure I could find success and loads of fun as a ghostwriter or cranking out grant proposals for worthy nonprofits. Is it too late to get my PhD and teach in a university? Maybe I should have been a physical therapist all along. Again, the Spirit pulls my attention back to her and repeats her refrain.

We have this one short, beautiful life, and I want to do it all, but it isn't all for me to do. It does not belong to me, that which belongs to you. And you cannot live the life I work with the Spirit to map out for myself. That won't stop me from peering into your corner of this world for some light window shopping of your life, imagining what mine might be like if I tried it on for a bit. The discipline for each of us is to learn that building castles in the sandboxes of our imagination brings creative thinking and problem-solving with a healthy side of escapism. Meanwhile, we look down the road and watch the builders of the actual castle hard at work, claiming the path that belongs to them and not ourselves.

"That house for me, David," God says, "that house belongs to someone else's work, their dream and destiny." Perhaps accepting this reality is among the most important shows of faithfulness: trusting that an idea or dream I cherish belongs to someone else's vocation. God clearly shows David and Moses where their work ends and another person's begins.

Our distractibility for the newest next leads us into three blunders if we are not careful. The first is missed sabbath time with God. For David and Moses, God wanted a break and to rest. Moses had done the work God had given him, and he needed to rest easy from his labors. For him, the final time of sabbath lies ahead. I love this scene from Deuteronomy—it always gives me goose bumps. God tends to Moses's death and buries him in a wholly unique show of affection and gratitude for Moses's faithfulness.

In David's case, I hear a desire to be left alone for a bit in God. God states how he has been present with his people from the time of Moses to this time of David, happily residing in a tent. I hear in this exchange a plea from God: Please don't fence me in. Not yet. Let me be wild and free a little longer. And you, David, need to take a break from your many campaigns and projects.

We, like David, find it challenging to sit still and be with our thoughts. It's with good reason that God said, "Be still, and know that I am God" (Psalm 46:10). The imperative at the beginning presents the most significant challenge and the most important. We have to fight against our culture's demands for productivity and against "laziness." I find it difficult to stop and do one thing; merely doing two presents enough of a challenge. Last month, my physical therapist joked about his "nothing" box, where he mentally goes to think about nothing. I can't conceive of that. Never has there been nothing in my mind. I hear God's command to "Be still" and leave the work for someone else as a plea to want to spend time with me, one I fail to answer all too often.

Not only do we miss potential sabbath time with God when we skip to the next, but we also risk creating roadblocks and potholes for those doing the work. When we step into work that belongs to someone else, our belief that we can do it better and more efficiently often has the opposite effect. We jump in to take over and get in the way of the excellent work currently accomplished by others. We inhibit the growth and ministry of others in our arrogant certainty we could do it better and have more valuable skills.

Finally, this compulsion to take up the newest shiny project distracts us from the one in progress, the one we began already with God's encouragement and blessing. As stated, I find the later middle and end of projects challenging. I grow bored with the work and want to move on. This word from the Spirit, "Not your time. Not your place. Not your call," turns me around to face the work that does belong to me. It pushes my attention back to that which God has called me and invited me to partner with him in accomplishing. If I stop and listen, I will remember the excitement I felt at the start of the existing project and find renewed motivation to see it complete.

Accepting the fact that God does not desire us to engage in every opportunity that pops into our minds comes slowly and painfully. I want to do it all and try everything. Is it my fault God created such a fascinating universe full of captivating personalities and projects?

With the Spirit's reminder comes the more difficult truth that perhaps distrust lies within the belly of my enthusiasm. What if the person called to that work does it incorrectly? What if they fail? Or what if it doesn't turn out as well as it could? There's not a tiny bit of ego in that distrust. God points to the promised land and tells Moses he will not enter. Moses must have had visions for what it could be and hopes for what the people might accomplish together. As people of hope, we can't help but project possible outcomes and dream of what might be. God tells Moses and David to set down the work and trust those that follow after. Accepting that we do not walk into the next phase of a goal for which we have worked leaves us heavy and unfulfilled at times.

I hear the Spirit's push once again: Not your time. Not your place. Not your call. This does not detract from the work that does belong to us. She does not admonish us for being unsuccessful or insufficient. Instead, she pulls us to see again our unique vocations and charismas, which belong to our story and no one else's. We do not look at Moses's death in the wilderness nor David's inability to construct the temple as failures. We see them both as human and having weaknesses and failings, but we do not view them as failures.

Neither are we, my friends. When an opportunity closes to us, may we remember that not everything is meant for each of us, and may we celebrate that work for which our heart sings.

WWJD? WWID?

WWJD entered the cultural milieu around the time I graduated high school. By college, I saw WWJD, an abbreviation for "What would Jesus do?" emblazoned on bracelets, T-shirts, hats, coffee mugs, and other portable and wearable paraphernalia. The slogan became popular, especially among the conservative evangelical Christian crowd, as a way not only to guide personal decision-making but also to identify one another in the wilds of the world. Spotting WWJD on someone's wrist helped identify their theological stance and likely denominational affiliation. I had a friend whose college professor thought it stood for "Who wants Jack Daniels?" certainly a livelier spin on the initials.

Recently, in articles and memes, I've seen people revisit the concept of asking oneself, "What would Jesus do?" before acting. The surface intention of the idea feels sound, a way of double-checking our compassionate hearts before letting our wilder emotions drive our behavior. Most of us prefer to think of the Jesus who heals the sick and lame, teaches endearing stories about seeds and wayward travelers, and pulls small children into his lap. That's the Jesus of Sunday school portraits and charming stained-glass windows.

But that doesn't represent the whole of Jesus of Nazareth. These recent reevaluations of WWJD point out that Jesus also threw over tables in a fit of rage, called his close friend Peter "Satan," and talked back to his mother. The Jesus who healed the ear of the man who came to arrest him feels more palatable of an example than the one who argued back with the Canaanite woman, calling her a "dog."

This old slogan came to mind the other day as I rode in the car with two of my children. I can't recall the topic of conversation, but we wandered into reflecting on how we make decisions. My middle child comfortably and confidently said, "I just ask, 'What would I do?'" I sat back in my seat, holding the wheel as a revelation washed over me. I told her she had really said something with those words.

"What would I do?" WWID?

Perhaps the question and answer come more easily to my middle because of her age, but I have to give her credit for being naturally self-assured and confident. She knows herself and feels good about how she behaves in the world, qualities too many of us have felt diminish as we age.

Most people second-guess themselves . . . or third or fourth. As I sit in middle age, I find myself passing through a more difficult era of feeling less sure about my abilities for discernment. Perhaps from our twenties into our forties, we feel a stronger compulsion to fit in and do as others believe rather than how we feel our heart leading us. Maybe not, but I seem to have many conversations with people in that age range who often ask, "What do you think I should do?"

Understandably, we feel compelled to seek the input of others. Some seek validation for their ability to make good decisions, some want affirmation that their choices are sound, and some genuinely distrust their own minds and hearts to lead them on a true path. It's okay to seek validation, and it's okay to feel uncertain at times.

WWJD feels good on the surface, but a deeper evaluation raises too many complications for comfort. It depends on which gospel we read and which version of Christ within that gospel we choose. Do we do as the Jesus of John's gospel, speaking in riddles and never quite fully engaging in others' human experience? Then again, the

Jesus of John's gospel kneels at the feet of his friends to tenderly wash them the night before his arrest and execution.

We could follow the Jesus of Mark, who rushes about, demanding secrecy, focused on his goal of the cross, and meeting each individual as they are, not concerned with the universal application of his teachings. But then we also meet Mark's Jesus preaching through enigmatic sayings like, "To you has been given the secret of the kingdom of God, but for those outside, everything comes in parables; so that 'they may indeed look, but not perceive, and may indeed listen, but not understand; so that they may not turn again and be forgiven." Does Jesus mean that he intentionally teaches in parables so people outside the group of his followers will not understand him?

Matthew and Luke come with other complications. We love the Jesus of the manger and wise men, the rabbi who preached the Sermon on the Mount, but we shy away from the one who says, "Do not think that I have come to bring peace to the earth. I have not come to bring peace but a sword. For I have come to set a man against his father, and a daughter against her mother, and a daughter-in-law against her mother-in-law. And a person's enemies will be those of his own household."

Aside from the more problematic behaviors and sayings of Jesus, we need to consider his unique calling as the Messiah. God sent Christ into the world with a particular purpose, one only he could complete. Asking ourselves, "WWJD?" fails to take this into account. We do not share an identical calling with Christ. We can try to show greater compassion and love to the world, as he did with his life and death. We can hear the lessons he left behind and apply them to our lives. However, a wholesale application of his behavior as an absolute template for our own would be impossible and inappropriate. God does not call each of us to be the Messiah.

WWID? What would I do?

Whether or not she intentionally chose it, my middle child's word choice matters. "What would I do?" demands a different perspective than "What should I do?" The latter starts with an assessment of expectations and rules placed upon us. "Should" begs us to consider how our friends, family, society, culture, and community view certain behaviors and choices. Asking, "What would I do?" starts inside our minds and hearts to consider our inclinations before the preferences of others.

If I ask myself, "What should I do?" I imagine any number of close friends or family members and how they would respond. I might ask them the same question for advice and counsel, unsure of my ability to think clearly and rightly about any situation. "What would I do?" turns our focus inwards as though we offer advice to ourselves. When someone asks our opinion, we regularly begin our answer with, "If I were you, I would . . ." "What would I do?" puts us in the double seat of both counseled and counselor. It moves us a step back for a slightly more objective view.

The question also identifies our innate capacities and gifts. WWID recognizes my individual persona, including the unique combination of gifts God granted me and no one else in my immediate community. I do not share the same calling as you, as my children, my parents, or as Jesus. The Spirit guides me to explore different paths open to me and no one else because of this unique identity as a beloved child of God.

We ask WWJD, in a worthy and noble endeavor, to place our viewpoint in that of our faith. We plant our decision-making in the tradition of Christ, paying heed to his teachings and examples. But we, too, must temper this with WWID, taking into account our vocation and discipleship, rooted in the Spirit's guidance and gifts singular to ourselves.

Bob Ross and Waiting to Understand Jesus

"Jesus answered, 'You do not know now what I am doing, but later you will understand.'"

- John 13:7

The above might be the most helpful thing Jesus says in all of John's Gospel. At times, he says things profound, divine, deeply spiritual, and thought-provoking. But other times, what comes out of his mouth is downright confusing. He spoke the above words to his disciples, but they still hold truth for us today. Despite reading multiple commentaries on specific selections, I find that portions of John's Gospel continue to make little sense to me. At such times, I hold onto St. Paul's words, "For now we see in a mirror, dimly, but then we will see face to face. Now I know only in part; then I will know fully, even as I have been fully known." (I Corinthians 13:12)

For Proper 14, Year B, churches following the Revised Common Lectionary read John 6:35, 41-51, a passage filled with enigmatic sayings to a confused audience. Honestly, I can't blame the people listening who, at the beginning of the selection, question Jesus's authority to speak as he does. I would be more inclined to question why he speaks the way he does. They see him as Mary's and Joseph's kid, whom they have known for years and who now claims to have come down from heaven. They know his story and know his parents; his claim to have come from elsewhere directly contradicts their lived experience of him. Of course, they question his words and meaning.

The Jesus of John loves to speak in riddles with little intention of providing the solution when his listeners grow weary of trying to solve them. His words in this passage have me scratching my head: "No one can come to me unless drawn by the Father who sent me, and I will raise that person up on the last day. It is written in the prophets, 'And they shall all be taught by God.' Everyone who has heard and learned from the Father comes to me. Not that anyone has seen the Father except the one who is from God; he has seen the Father." What is the "last day," as Jesus means it, not as we have interpreted it over millennia? And what of this clarification that people who hear and learn from the Father come to Jesus, but no one has seen the Father "except the one who is from God"? We assume he speaks of himself, and the rest of us only hear and learn from God but cannot see God. However, is that accurate? I try to lean on the thousands of scholars who have come before me, but this version of Jesus challenges my willingness to accept the church's standard interpretation blanketly.

The wonderful thing is that I don't have to; I neither have to accept others' interpretations nor have a fully conceived one of my own. As we endeavor for theological understanding and divine relationship, we all are works in progress. The other day, I sat, waiting for my middle to finish her last (yay!) orthodontist appointment, and watched reruns on the waiting room television. I love our orthodontist for my two older kids for many reasons, including the fact she does not force people to watch news channels or listen to Christian pop music. Instead, she streams old and new PBS shows, and I leave her waiting room calmer and more informed than when I entered.

For this, on my last visit to her office, I enjoyed the calming voice, large hair, and singular artistic stylings of Bob Ross. I feel sorry for you if you do not know whom I mean. Though he passed away in 1995 at the young age of 52, his star shines on thanks to local PBS stations and newer streaming services. I think his show continues to amass a cult following, primarily due to his quiet, patient ways. The fact that he sports a giant afro, classic 70s blue jeans, and a fabulous beard to match also helps.

I sat enthralled as Bob pulled paint from his pallet, a classic Ross move, not with a brush but a pallet knife. He dotted paint across his canvas with no apparent rhyme or reason. I cocked my head sideways like a Labrador upon hearing an imperceptible sound. What could he possibly be painting? At this point in the process, I could envision birds, a tree, water, a fishing pole, really almost anything. He chatted calmly and quietly, not providing too many hints of his intention, but moved his pallet knife deliberately from pallet to canvas.

At this point in his work, I began to understand that had I been the creator in this scenario, I probably would have thrown away the canvas. No way could those dabs of paint and smears of color turn into anything but a hot mess. The composition lacked any clear direction. I crave to see progress in the moment that points to my intended goal; I need apparent order and a plan that spans ahead of me like train tracks.

Not Bob. He knew the vision in his mind and trusted his years of practicing the craft he loved, despite the tremendous criticism he received for his unique style and technique. He trusted his own process, patiently trudging through each imperceptible step. "Trudging" isn't the right word. He . . . skipped? No, that's too jaunty. Lumbered? Nope, too heavy and careless. Delightedly stepped? That's wrong, too. Though delight clearly shows in Ross's demeanor, the word feels too light and spontaneous. He proceeds confidently and unhurried with conscious movement towards his goal. He never worries or panics, even when he makes a mistake. Famously, he said, "We don't make mistakes; we have happy accidents."

Eventually, his smears and dabs transformed into a mountain range reflected on the water below. For the first ten minutes of the video, I would have argued with anyone who said that would be the result. Halfway into it, none of my assumptions held, and I could only watch, transfixed, to see what this peaceful, unharried, and unhurried man would do.

By the time I walked out the door with my smiling teenager, Bob Ross had reminded me never to give up, especially not halfway through when you cannot see nor discern a reasonably successful outcome. That process is much like my children's wearing braces. You wonder how the rubber bands, brackets, chains, and wires could produce polished white smiles one to one and a half years in. You forget what they looked like before the braces and cannot imagine them after. The smile stays in your mind, a jumble of grey metal hunks and lines. Then they walk out of the long-awaited removal appointment, and there they stand before you, utterly transformed from the hour before. They open their mouths wide in the lines of a waxing moon, and your smile blooms even wider across your face.

Faith is like that; reading the Bible is like that; relating to Jesus is like that. Sometimes, I love the words of Jesus, and excitement wells inside me at the blessing of preaching or writing about the Gospel. Other times, I feel I'm halfway through a Bob Ross episode, wondering how anything will come of Jesus's jumble of words and smeared dollops of meaning, and I've watched all of Jesus's episodes many times before. I scratch my head and wonder either, "What did Jesus mean?" or, more often, "Jesus didn't really mean that."

I try not to worry too much when I trip on passages and can't find my way. That requires first giving up the temptation and illusion that I should or do have an answer for every question regarding God, Jesus, the Bible, and Christianity. As a priest, I continue to battle that demon of the ego rather than accepting the reality of my humanity, including my dark and cloudy lens, of which Paul speaks.

Jesus told his disciples they wouldn't understand what he did for them or what he said, but one day, they would. Later, the truth may wash over them, but we hear this promise in the context of a messiah who promises eternal life. "Later" can be a long time. I lean into the mystery of it and read interpretations on particularly enigmatic pericopes with a hearty balance of skepticism and acceptance. The best scholars fall victim to the limitations of their lenses, the same as I do.

As confusing as I find the bulk of the passage, I stand alongside millions of my fellow Christians, feeling comfort by the end: "Very truly, I tell you, whoever believes has eternal life. I am the bread of life. Your ancestors ate the manna in the wilderness, and they died. This is the bread that comes down from heaven so that one may eat of it and not die. I am the living bread that came down from heaven. Whoever eats of this bread will live forever, and the bread that I will give for the life of the world is my flesh."

Jesus does not say that the one who understands every word and solves his riddles experiences eternal life and enjoys the soul-nourishing bread only he provides. He says those belong to people who come to eat and drink. Our understanding deepens with our experience, not the other way around. God requires no answers in order for us to come to the table, asks for no credentials, nor presents any test to pass. Instead, Christ issues an invitation to come, eat and drink, be fed by God's wisdom, and then grow in wisdom ourselves, however limited.

I don't need the answers; I only need to come forward with the questions.

A Dragonfly's Wings

"Mom, did you know a dragonfly can flap its wings in opposite directions? It's the only animal that can do that. That's why it can fly like a helicopter and hover."

My morning and afternoon car rides with my kids regularly include a number of "fun facts," as my son calls them. Between my three children, our hours spent driving from place to place comprise the primary source of my continuing education these days. I attended excellent schools all the way through earning my master's degree, and yet my children continue to add to my knowledge. I don't remember which kid filled me in on the unique nature of dragonfly wings, but I responded truthfully that I did not know that.

I delight in the fact God created us as perpetual students. My father tells the story of his first year in medical school when a professor fed a fellow student a much-needed slice of humble pie. My dad recalls that the student raised his hand to eagerly answer every question the professor proffered. After months of this, the professor grew annoyed, finally proclaiming, "Bill, it's not what you don't know that's your problem; it's what you don't know you don't know." Indeed.

I often find myself drawn to Matthew 18:1-3: "At that time, the disciples came to Jesus and asked, 'Who is the greatest in the kingdom of heaven?' He called a child, whom he put among them, and said, 'Truly I tell you, unless you change and become like children, you will never enter the kingdom of heaven.'" This verse resonates with me, reminding me of the beauty of childhood curiosity. In its purest form, childhood is a time of play and uninhibited being, a time when every discovery is a wonder.

Small children point to the world with the ever-present "What's that?" on their lips. They discover with amazement everyday items adults take for granted. Long ago, before I had kids, I attended a Pampered Chef party and won an avocado peeler as a door prize. This simple tool has a black handle and a rounded metal end, slightly bent to slide between a ripe avocado's peel and flesh. When my oldest grew big enough to open the drawer full of kitchen utensils, she found this shiny metal object with a smooth plastic part ideally suited to her little hands. She did not let go for months. The peeler went with us to the grocery store and restaurants on car rides and vacations. I tried to ignore the fact that from a distance, it appeared we had armed our toddler with a kitchen knife. To my oldest, the avocado peeler had nothing to do with a mushy green fruit and everything to do with comfort and wonder.

Since another child informed me of the unique nature of dragonfly wings, I now spot them everywhere. They dart through our front yard, even though no body of water sits near our house. My friend's father was the world's leading expert on dragonflies and named several species after his wife. As I watch the black ones with blue-tipped wings zoom around, I think of him and find his gesture romantic.

My child's words echo through my mind as I watch these winged wonders. A quick search for "dragonfly" takes me down a rabbit hole of information, including that dragonflies date back to the early Jurassic period. One of these ancestors holds the title for the largest insect to have ever lived at roughly thirty inches long. They cover every continent except Antarctica. Their lacy wings fascinate me, as do their impossibly thin bodies. Many resemble a toothpick with a raisin and lace stuck on one end. And yet, these seemingly fragile blades carry their bodies in daring patterns of flight.

If a dragonfly can take us deep into a well of research for fascinating facts and new information, imagine what the whole of the universe holds. We cannot comprehend but a fraction of a fraction of all of God's creation. To become like a child includes forgetting we know so much and, instead, look at the created world with eyes full of wonder, a mind eager for knowledge, and a heart hungry to understand, from the largest planetary body to the smallest molecule under a microscope. The mitochondria alone present a depth of information we have yet been able to plumb fully.

Author Anne Lamott has captured her unique view of the world in nearly two dozen books over the years, sharing her stories with often raw candor and more than a little sense of humor. One of my favorites of hers summarizes the three most essential prayers as "Help. Thanks. Wow." which is the book's name. We often remember the first two but miss the third. The "Wow" grabs my attention both as a reminder and a conviction. In First Corinthians, Paul instructs his readers to "glory in the Lord" (1 Corinthians 1:31). Some translations render the same text, "boast in the Lord," but I first heard it in the King James Version, and it stays in my mind as such. I like "glory" better. It feels contradictory to "boast." When I think of glorying in something, I think to bask in it, delight in it, and revel and wonder in it— "wow" in it.

I want to wonder more, wow more, and step out into God's creation with less assumption and more amazement. I want to forget that I know so much and remember that I am a child of God, no matter my age, and still have much to learn. I want the world to thrill and easily impress me because I have this one life, and the world contains more than I will ever know.

I want to sit and watch a dragonfly perch precariously on a blade of grace, wonder how she does it, and then wonder more about the one who created her. The dragonfly, with its unique wings and graceful flight, serves as a reminder of the wonder and beauty of God's creation, inspiring me to delve deeper into my faith and understanding of Her work.

Acknowledgments

This book is a culmination of my personal and professional journey, spanning more than twenty years as an Episcopal priest, over sixteen years as a mother, and a lifetime of love for cooking. I am deeply grateful for the congregations I have served and those where I have been a guest preacher. The wisdom and life experiences shared by the people in these churches have enriched me and significantly influenced my personal growth and writing process.

I could not have finished this project without the help and inspiration of my many fellow writers and clergy. They happily sat for hours as I fleshed out my ideas, reached back into my archives for material, asked their opinions, and gave their valuable time to read my manuscript and provide suggestions and encouragement. I especially thank the women of the Valle Crucis Conference Center Women Writers. I leave my weekends with them rejuvenated and inspired, thanks to our leader, Katerina Katsarka Whitley, and the incredible answers the women write for her prompts. She also edits all of my printed work, serving her suggestions with a side of Greek love and, often, food.

I am profoundly grateful for my family, whose unwavering encouragement and inspiration have been a constant source of strength in my writing journey. My children bring me joy and daily challenges, which I cherish and could not live without. Derek, their father, has been a supportive co-parent, friend, and neighbor, always cheering me on and gracefully navigating the parenting journey with me. His role as my brainstorming partner and first reader for my works has been invaluable. My parents and brother continue to be a pillar of support, as they have been throughout my more than four decades on this planet.

And then there's Gigi, who keeps me nourished, ensures I stretch, brings me something to drink while I'm writing because she knows I've forgotten, and enriches my life in countless ways. Her smile and her candidness inspire me to share writing that I might otherwise keep to myself and prevent me from publishing anything that misses the mark. She brings magic to even the most ordinary, mundane days.

Index
Reflections by Theme

Gratitude and Thanksgiving
Gratitude in Offering	51
Consider the Dandelion	55
Enzymes and Hospitality	62
Hope in the Face of a Ring Bearer	66
Savor	78
A Dragonfly's Wings	113

Joy in Faith
The Seriousness of the Youngest Disciples	6
For the Sport of It	11
Loving the Story, Inspiring Play	92
A Dragonfly's Wings	113

Loss
For Rosemary	25
Jesus Wept, So Why Can't We?	48

Personal Faithfulness
Extraordinarily Ordinary	1
The Seriousness of the Youngest Disciples	6
The Prodigal and the Pigs	15
Prayer in the Kitchen	20
God the Father and Father's Day…It's Complicated.	31
The Error in Fundamentals	34
Faith in Stitches	45
The Unbearable, Relatable All-Or-Nothing of Peter	82

Prayer
For the Sport of It	11
Prayer in the Kitchen	20
Homemade Butter and the Drip, Dripping of Sabbath Time	41

Questions and Wonder
The Seriousness of the Youngest Disciples	6
For the Sport of It	11
Bob Ross and Waiting to Understand Jesus	107
A Dragonfly's Wings	113

Relationships
The Prodigal and the Pigs	15
God the Father and Father's Day…It's Complicated.	31
Sacrificing Busyness	37
Enzymes and Hospitality	62
Hope in the Face of a Ring Bearer	66
Bumper Cars and Spider Webs	74
Savor	78
WWJD? WWID?	103

Sabbath Keeping
Prayer in the Kitchen	20
Sacrificing Busyness	37
Homemade Butter and the Drip, Dripping of Sabbath Time	41
I'm Sorry, I Can't.	70
Savor	78
Not Your Time. Not Your Place. Not Your Call.	96

Scriptural Reflections
For the Sport of It	11
The Prodigal and the Pigs	15
God the Father and Father's Day…It's Complicated.	31
A Good Word Not for Me	86
Loving the Story, Inspiring Play	92
Not Your Time. Not Your Place. Not Your Call.	96

Trust
The Error in Fundamentals	34

Consider the Dandelion	55
Standing in My Sun	58
Hope in the Face of a Ring Bearer	66
The Unbearable, Relatable All-Or-Nothing of Peter	82
WWJD? WWID?	103
Bob Ross and Waiting to Understand Jesus	107

Vocation and Discipleship

Extraordinarily Ordinary	1
Homemade Butter and the Drip, Dripping of Sabbath Time	41
Consider the Dandelion	55
Standing in My Sun	58
Enzymes and Hospitality	62
I'm Sorry, I Can't.	70
A Good Word Not for Me	86
Not Your Time. Not Your Place. Not Your Call.	96
WWJD? WWID?	103

About the Author

Mary R. Hemmer lives in northeast Georgia with her family, where she helps tend the family farm, writes for her blog prayerfulkitchen.substack.com, leads workshops and retreats, and guest preaches at area churches most Sundays. You can find her on most social media outlets by her handle @prayerfulkitchen. She has one other book available in print, *Phe and the Work of Death*, written under the name Mary R. H. Demmler. She also contributed to the book *In the Beginning Was The Word: An Anthology,* edited by Katerina Katsarka Whitley. She loves that no two days are alike for her, but hopes most of them find her in the kitchen, writing, or spending time with her three children—preferably all three!

www.ingramcontent.com/pod-product-compliance
Lightning Source LLC
Chambersburg PA
CBHW052146070526
44585CB00017B/1994